★ ⬛HOW TO BE *Ferocious* LIKE ★
S ⬛R ALEX FERGUSON

Hits & Memories of the
Human Hairdryer: the Tantrums,
the Tirades, the Trophies

GLENN CONNLEY

Marshall Cavendish
Editions

© 2011 Marshall Cavendish International (Asia) Private Limited

Published by Marshall Cavendish Editions
An imprint of Marshall Cavendish International
1 New Industrial Road, Singapore 536196

Other Marshall Cavendish Offices: Marshall Cavendish International. PO Box 65829, London EC1P 1NY, UK • Marshall Cavendish Corporation. 99 White Plains Road, Tarrytown NY 10591-9001, USA • Marshall Cavendish International (Thailand) Co Ltd. 253 Asoke, 12th Flr, Sukhumvit 21 Road, Klongtoey Nua, Wattana, Bangkok 10110, Thailand • Marshall Cavendish (Malaysia) Sdn Bhd, Times Subang, Lot 46, Subang Hi-Tech Industrial Park, Batu Tiga, 40000 Shah Alam, Selangor Darul Ehsan, Malaysia.

Marshall Cavendish is a trademark of Times Publishing Limited

National Library Board, Singapore Cataloguing-in-Publication Data

Connley, Glenn, 1972-
How to be ferocious like Sir Alex Ferguson : hits & memories of the human hairdryer : the tantrums, the tirades, the trophies / Glenn Connley. — Singapore : Marshall Cavendish Editions, c2011.
p. cm.
ISBN : 978-981-4346-67-2 (pbk.)

1. Ferguson, Alex, 1941- 2. Manchester United (Soccer team)
3. Soccer managers — England — Manchester — Biography.
4. Soccer managers — Scotland — Biography. I. Title.

GV942.7
796.334092 -- dc22   OCN728081498

Printed in Singapore by Times Printers

contents

A JOCK FROM THE DOCK

> A bunch of Glaswegians arrive at the Pearly Gates and God instructs St Peter to let in only the most virtuous of the group.
>
> A few minutes later, a breathless St Peter returns to God and announces: "They're gone!"
>
> God replies: "What, all of them?"
>
> "No," says St Peter "… the Pearly Gates!"

In the winter of 1942 the shipbuilding district of Scotland's biggest city, Glasgow, spawned the country's best-known funny man — and author of the above joke — Billy Connolly.

Eleven months earlier, just a few streets away, it delivered a slightly less comedic champion, but one who nonetheless achieved his own brand of world domination: Manchester United's record-breaking manager, Sir Alex Ferguson.

These days, one is known for his animated, expletive-laden stand-up routines… the other is a bearded comedian.

Alexander Chapman Ferguson is one of football's most divisive and polarising figures. He is adored by United's legion of fans around the world, said to number some 350 million, after delivering the club an unprecedented generation of accomplishment which continues to this day.

Yet the man known universally as "Fergie" has made more than his fair share of enemies along the way.

In spite of all his success, he is football's biggest grouch. There are millions of football followers of the non-Manchester United persuasion who would say they dislike — even hate — Ferguson.

If you cross his path you'll get a serve. It doesn't matter whether you're a player, a manager, a national icon or an entire nation. Fergie's only form of defence is attack:

> Kenny Dalglish has associates but only a few friends. There's nothing wrong with that because, at the end of the day, you only need six people to carry your coffin.
>
> – SIR ALEX FERGUSON

> When you do bad things he still wants to kill you.
>
> – ARSENE WENGER

> **They say he's (Arsene Wenger) an intelligent man, right? Speaks five languages? I've got a 15-year-old boy from the Ivory Coast who speaks five languages.**
>
> **– SIR ALEX FERGUSON**

Understanding Sir Alex requires a basic introduction to the district into which he was born. It goes a long way to explaining his combative demeanour and explosive temper.

Glasgow's inner eastern dockside was an intimidating place in post-war Britain. The area had a unique language, code and honour system. To this day, Fergie almost single-handedly attributes his success to the tough, occasionally brutal, adolescence he spent on the banks of the Clyde River in the 1940s and '50s.

It was a time when Glasgow was one of the world's great industrial powers. The shipyards are long gone today. So are the childhood tenement homes of "the Big Yin" and Fergie.

Connolly often jokes that nowadays the Clyde River runs through Glasgow because "it would be mugged if it walked".

> **The great thing about Glasgow now is that if there is a nuclear attack, it'll look exactly the same afterwards.**
>
> **– BILLY CONNOLLY**

Sir Alex is a little more circumspect with his nostalgia.

"Anybody who has grown up in the shadow of the derelict yards that came to litter the banks of the river cannot possibly imagine the clamour and vitality they brought to the streets of my childhood," Ferguson wrote in his 1999 autobiography, *Managing My Life*.

The multi-million pound mansion which Sir Alex now shares with his wife Lady Cathy in Wilmslow, Cheshire, is named Fairfields, in memory of the shipyard where his father spent the bulk of his working life.

> I was born in the shadow of the Fairfield crane
> Where the blast of a freighter's horn
> Was the very first sound that reached my ears
> On the morning I was born
> – The Fairfield Crane, by Archie Fisher

On New Year's Eve 1941, Alex Ferguson was born on the floor of his grandmother's house in Govan, two and a half miles south-west of Glasgow's city centre. His parents' home, just a few hundred yards from Ibrox stadium, remained the centrepiece of his family life until he moved his own young family to Aberdeen thirty-six and a half years later.

"Any success I have had in handling men — and especially in creating a culture of loyalty and commitment in teams I have managed — owes much to my upbringing among the working men of Clydeside," he recalls.

① Ferguson's Childhood Home
667 Govan Road

② Ferguson's Birth Place
357 Shieldhall Road

③ Ibrox Stadium
Home of Rangers FC

④ Billy Connolly's Birth Place
69 Dover Street

Like Connolly, Ferguson has a mouth like a Glaswegian wharfie.

He may be a knight of the realm, but Fergie's not averse to dropping the occasional 'F-bomb'. You don't have to be a lip reader to know what he's saying when the cameras cut to him on the sidelines during a Manchester United match if things aren't going according to plan.

Again, just like Connolly, Ferguson's acid tongue has landed him in hot water on numerous occasions.

> My greatest challenge was knocking Liverpool right off their fucking perch. And you can print that.
> – SIR ALEX FERGUSON, *The Guardian*, 2002

> Just fucking patch him up.
> – SIR ALEX FERGUSON (After kicking a boot into David Beckham's head)

But more on that later.

The young Alex Ferguson could already handle himself.

He recalls a host of schoolyard and street skirmishes from which he usually came out on top, albeit with the odd bloodied nose or split lip.

At the age of ten or eleven he was bullied by a couple of older lads in a snooker hall. Believe it or not, he was fooled into drinking urine by the big boys. But, in typical Fergie fashion, he would have the last laugh. Waiting outside the door for his opportunity, he pelted his tormentors with billiard balls, smashing one on the jaw — an injury which was still bandaged up weeks later. Talk about taking the piss!

While the Ferguson household was as loving and nurturing as any you'd find today, it was no walk in the park.

As a child, Sir Alex admits tormenting his little brother Martin, who is a year younger. On one such occasion, though, it was Alex who came off second-best. He had to be rushed to hospital suffering a severe burn on his thigh after Martin responded to his taunts by branding him with a coal poker from the living room fireplace. Food for thought for rival managers, no doubt.

Despite winning a shed-load of trophies and earning millions of pounds in his years since moving to England, Sir Alex still claims to be a Glaswegian at heart. In an interview with Sir David Frost in 2008 he declared he could still walk down the streets of Govan and be accepted as a local. He insists his very best friends are not those from the world of football, but from his childhood.

"Two of my closest pals, Duncan Petersen and Jim McMillan, were with me in the local nursery when we were four. Duncan remembers being in the bed next to me when we were put down for a wee sleep in the afternoons. All three of us are still in regular touch with other mates, including Tommy Hendry, who played with us in Life Boys football. Tommy ranks as a latecomer because we didn't know him until he was five and a half. It seems natural to us that connections made back then have lasted more than fifty years."

At Govan High School one (possibly psychic) teacher described him as "confrontational and aggressive" in a school report. It's fair to say he's never quite managed to shake off those attributes.

Fergie claims to have worked hard as a student. But he made a much bigger name for himself on Govan High's football pitch than he ever did in any of the classrooms. At the age of sixteen, and secretly harbouring dreams of a career in football, he followed the well-trodden Glasgow path and quit school to begin an apprenticeship on the docks.

He began his working life as a tool-maker with the Wickman Group, a company which produced carbon-tipped tools such as industrial lathes. After a year he made his first tactical transfer. With redundancies pending at Wickman, he moved to the nearby Remington Rand typewriter manufacturer.

It was at Remington where he first laid eyes on a pretty new office worker by the name of Cathy Holding. Ever the romantic, Fergie noted she "had a lovely walk and a nice bum". Frighteningly, he said something similar about Ryan Giggs when he first saw him play as a kid thirty years later.

On the morning of March 12, 1966 (it had to be in the morning, Alex was playing football in the afternoon), Alex and Cathy were married in Glasgow's Martha Street Registry Office. They weren't able to have a church wedding because Fergie was Protestant and Cathy was Catholic.

While rushing for photos after the ceremony, he impressed his new bride no end when he "lost his rag" and started shouting at someone who tried to pinch his parking spot outside the photographer's studio.

"Cathy was not too pleased. Good start, Alex," is how he recalls his first foray into married life.

There was no honeymoon, either... well, not for Cathy anyway. Fergie went to Spain with his Dunfermline teammates to play against Real Zaragoza in the Fairs Cup (the precursor to today's Europa League) just a few days later. Cathy stayed home in Glasgow.

And so for almost half a century Cathy Ferguson has played second fiddle to a bunch of sweating, grunting, spitting men — most of whom are about a third of her husband's age. To her, the football scores serve as little more than a guide to anticipate Sir Alex's mood when, eventually, he arrives home from "that stupid game".

"I have to respect my wife because she's not a football fan," Fergie told Frost. "When our games are on TV she doesn't watch them."

Sir Alex has often joked that Lady Cathy "wears the pants" in the Ferguson household. He consults her on most of the big decisions about his career. In 2002, it was Cathy who talked him out of retiring as manager of Manchester United.

> In 2002, I made the decision on a whim. The age 60 sounded good. On New Year's Eve, we went out for dinner and when we came back I fell asleep on the couch. My wife, Cathy, came in with the three boys behind her. She kicked my foot and said, 'You are not retiring'!
>
> **– SIR ALEX FERGUSON**

If the fans at Old Trafford didn't already love Cathy Ferguson before that, her unselfish act (or was she simply protecting her own sanity?) endeared her to the United fans even more.

During the 2002-03 title-winning season, a new chant reverberated around Old Trafford, a chant which began the week after Fergie announced he (actually, she) had changed his mind about abdicating his Old Trafford throne.

> Oh, every single one of us,
> Loves Cathy Ferguson,
> Loves Cathy Ferguson,
> Loves Cathy Ferguson.
> – Manchester United fans, 2002

FATHER KNOWS BEST

You don't have to look far to discover where Fergie inherited his famously ferocious temper and impatient, gruff nature.

Alex Ferguson Senior was a complicated, highly principled — if somewhat silent — man. (Clearly, Junior didn't inherit *all* those traits.)

"One of my persistent memories is of him sitting by the fire for hours, silently reading, but when his temper blew it could be like a volcano. I usually contrived to be out of the way of the consequences, leaving Martin to take the brunt of Dad's anger."

As a 12 year old, Alex Junior couldn't resist a wee peek at his father's pay packet and was shocked to discover that for working up to seventy hours on the docks, his old man received a meagre £7 per week. It was that moment which cemented Junior's "determination to make something of myself".

When he was a teenager in the mid 1950s, Fergie was playing football for Queens Park and would often find himself pitted against men twice his age.

He once described a match against a team from Eaglesham, just south of the city, as being made up of eleven giant blacksmiths on a pitch resembling a paddy field. It was boys against men and the tall, skinny centre forward was battered by mammoth opposition defenders.

When he arrived home in Govan after the game he described the scene to his father. These days, modern dads might be outraged if sons were clobbered by men twice their age and size. Not Alex Ferguson Senior. "It will do you the world of good. If you can't take it, don't play it."

Earlier, when Fergie's football talents started to attract publicity, his father was worried the attention might go to his son's head. A glowing profile in the *Govan Press* triggered a hostile reception from opposition fans when Govan High met arch rival St Gerard's Catholic Secondary School in the Whitefield Cup.

But, in the face of verbal abuse from grown men (yes, they were doing it 55 years ago), Alex senior refused to defend his son. "Dad was completely unmoved. Merely said that the only appropriate answer was to play well in the replay, preferably with a hat trick thrown in."

Sure enough, in the second leg Little Fergie scored three times in a 6—3 victory and couldn't resist celebrating right in front of the opposition fans.

"Dad was right about the best way to shut them up."

How to be Ferocious like Fergie:

Never take a backward step. If someone hoodwinks you into drinking piss, break their jaw with a billiard ball — they won't do it again. But be wary of brothers wielding red-hot poking irons.

Get your priorities right. Don't let unimportant stuff like marriage or honeymoons get in the way of football. Even if your future wife does have a nice bum.

Remember, the pen may be mightier than the sword... but the tongue can be even more lethal. Regardless of whether you're totally wrong about something and you know it, attack, attack, attack. "Youse are fucking idiots," Fergie famously told journalists who dared to criticise a dud player he'd just wasted 28 million quid on.

Never take
a backward step.
If someone
hoodwinks you into drinking piss,
↘**BREAK THEIR JAW**
with a billiard ball

GOD-GIVEN TALENT

Sir Alex Ferguson is often tendered as Exhibit A in the long-running argument that only average players become great managers.

Columnists and bloggers regularly lump him in with the likes of Jose Mourinho, Arsene Wenger and Sven Goran-Eriksson as managers whose playing careers were, at best, modest.

On the other side of the ledger are superstar players like Paul Ince, Bryan Robson, Bobby Moore and Sir Bobby Charlton, who were never comfortable in the managerial hot seat.

Fergie fits into neither of those categories.

Journalists who dismiss his playing days tend to rely on — and quote — each other. It's true he was no Kenny Dalglish or Denis Law, but it would be a travesty to write him off as an ordinary player.

If you'd never seen him play and had to guess what kind of player he was, you'd imagine him to have been a dour defender. You'd be wrong. In fact, Fergie was a fine striker with an amazing eye for goal, mixed with the toughness you'd expect in an old-fashioned Scottish centre forward.

His playing career ended prematurely — no question — but that's largely because of his hankering to become a manager. He turned down frequent offers to move to big clubs in England during his 16 years as a player. In Brando parlance, he truly "*coulda been a contender*" in the big leagues, but chose to remain in his native Scotland.

Hindsight is a wonderful tool for armchair experts. Looking back, his playing career pales into insignificance beside the pile of glittering silverware he's collected as a manager.

Whose wouldn't? But to ignore his playing days is to do him a great disservice.

His success as a manager has not come in spite of his playing career; it is an extension of it.

Alexander Ferguson – Playing Career			
YEARS	CLUB	GAMES	GOALS
1957–60	Queens Park	31	15
1960–64	St. Johnstone	37	19
1964–67	Dunfermline Athletic	89	66
1967–69	Rangers	41	25
1969–73	Falkirk	95	36
1973–74	Ayr United	24	9
	TOTALS	317	170

On the first of February 2010, at the age of 68, Sir Alex Ferguson returned to Govan High School as the guest of honour to mark its centenary.

A day earlier, he'd been swearing and chewing his way up and down the touchline at the Emirates Stadium in north London, as Manchester United hammered Arsenal 3—1 to draw within a point of eventual Premier League champions, Chelsea.

At his old school he received a welcome fit for a king. During his regal walk-about he was shown a black and white photograph of himself taken more than half a century earlier, wearing the number 10 of the school's senior football team.

"I still remember my time on the school Under-16 football team vividly. We won the Whitefield Cup, the Castle Cup and the Under-15 Cup," he told wide-eyed students.

Despite having played with — and coached — thousands of young footballers in the intervening years, he impressed his old alma mater even further by naming every single member of that team of 1956... off the top of his head.

It revealed an extraordinary talent which proves that although he's always been a workaholic, he has a rare football gift which sets him apart from the rest. To match his bear-like temper, he has the memory of an elephant.

It is somewhat ironic then that the genesis of his brilliance as a student of football is a direct result of his failure as a student in the classroom, after being held back from starting at Govan High with the rest of his pals.

He became depressed and introverted. He would later confess there were occasions he found life "so miserable that it might have done me permanent damage. Ultimately I was able to use those bad times to fuel the drive that carried me forward in later years".

Conversely, his feats on the football pitch as a schoolboy made him a "minor hero" to his classmates. On top of his tremendous athleticism, young Alex Ferguson was an astute tactician with an eye for spotting the weaknesses of a rival team.

In addition to playing for his school, he played for his church team and his local district club. If that wasn't enough, he somehow found time to sneak into Ibrox (sometimes against his father's wishes) to see his beloved Rangers, and dreamed of one day wearing the famous blue strip.

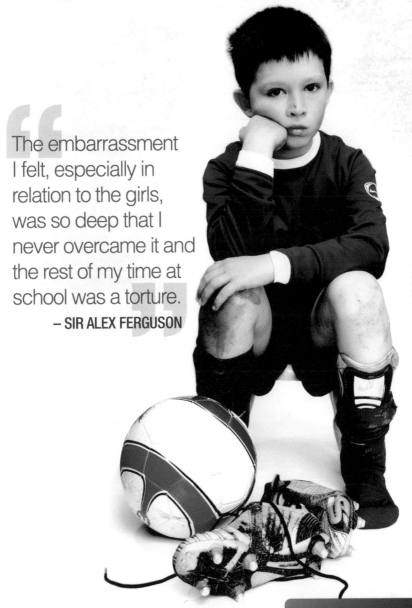

"The embarrassment I felt, especially in relation to the girls, was so deep that I never overcame it and the rest of my time at school was a torture.
– SIR ALEX FERGUSON

FACTFILE

QUEENS PARK FOOTBALL CLUB
FOUNDED 1867
HOME: HAMPDEN PARK, GLASGOW
CHAMPIONSHIPS: 2
SCOTTISH CUPS: 10 (ONLY RANGERS AND
CELTIC HAVE WON MORE)

Queens Park is Scotland's oldest Associated Football Club. It has retained its amateur status to this day, long after rival clubs were seduced by the mighty pound. Sadly — perhaps inevitably — the club has tumbled into the lowest division of Scottish football.

But that wasn't always the case for the proud club which has its home base at Scotland's national stadium, Hampden Park. It was here that Alex Ferguson's playing career took off... despite a somewhat inauspicious debut.

His baptism into the first eleven at the age of sixteen was memorable for all the wrong reasons. He described it as "a nightmare". After taking a train to Scotland's south-western tip to play Stranraer, Fergie started the game in an unfamiliar position on the right wing. He was crunched in an early collision with an opposition defender. As the pair were getting up Ferguson was flabbergasted when, as he put it, "the bastard bit me!"

At half time he was given a verbal shellacking by his manager for a perceived lack of aggression.

"You don't sidestep players at this club. You go through them. You've come into this team with a big reputation. What's the matter with you?

– JACKIE GARDINER

"The left back bit me.

– SIR ALEX FERGUSON

"Bit you? Then bite him back!

– JACKIE GARDINER

After just one season with the 'Glorious Hoops' it was clear a professional career beckoned. In his second season at Hampden Park Fergie was approached by Newcastle United following an impressive performance in a youth international between Scotland and England at St James' Park. He rejected what would the first of many offers to move south to England, in favour of staying in Glasgow to continue his apprenticeship.

A season later, however, the opportunity of playing for a club with First Division ambitions proved too great and he signed for Second Division St Johnstone at the age of nineteen, despite a sneaking suspicion that "leaving Queens Park was a big mistake".

Ferguson was flabbergasted when, as he put it, ↘ "THE BASTARD BIT ME!"

FACTFILE

ST. JOHNSTONE FOOTBALL CLUB
FOUNDED 1884
HOME: MUIRTON PARK (1924-89),
MCDIARMID PARK (1989+)
CHAMPIONSHIPS: 7
SCOTTISH CUPS: 0

You can see why these days Sir Alex Ferguson gets frustrated with the diamond-clad pretty boys prancing around the English Premier League. When he first stepped into the big time with a (comparatively) big club, there were no Range Rovers or private jets. Any player brave — or stupid — enough to wear a diamond studded ear-ring would probably get a belting from his teammates.

Initially, Ferguson played as an amateur at St Johnstone. The only cash he received was to cover the cost of getting to and from the club's training ground in Perth, and often that was like getting blood from a stone. It meant he had to keep his day job in Glasgow and travel by public transport to training and matches.

He'd get out of bed at 6am to work at the Remington factory. At 4pm he'd catch a bus to a suburban train station, then a train into Glasgow Central. He'd then leap into a taxi for the hop over to the Buchanan Street main line station for the two-hour journey north. Then it was a taxi to Muirton Park in time for training at 7.30pm. He was rarely home before 1am on training nights.

It's important to note that while he was now in the big

time of Scottish football, he and many of his family and friends continued to support Rangers. It's a situation which exists today. Many Scots (including homegrown Scottish Premier League players) support their own team *and* either Rangers or Celitc; such is the dominance of the 'Old Firm' clubs.

Towards the end of his first season in Perth, Ferguson became a part-time professional to help support his family after illness prematurely ended his father's career in the shipyards. His sign-on fee was £300. (Not quite the £80,000,000 he sold Cristiano Ronaldo to Real Madrid for four decades later.) His salary was similar to his weekly wage at the factory, a job he continued despite the change in his football status.

In his second season, St Johnstone were promoted to the First Division. Fergie had never cemented a place in the Saints' senior team and was languishing in the reserves. He begged to be transferred to a new club in the hope of fresh start. But, on 21 December, 1963, he had a life-changing — almost religious — experience.

A series of injuries to first team regulars forced manager Bobby Brown to pick Fergie to play against his beloved Rangers at Ibrox. It was like a childhood dream come true with Ferguson, a life-long Rangers fan, scoring a remarkable hat-trick in a shock 3—2 win for St Johnstone.

Ferguson scored 37 times for St Johnstone before moving to Dunfermline, who were competing for top honours with Rangers and Celtic at the time. He became a full-time professional and was paid £27 per week plus an extra £14 if the club were top of the table. His reputation continued to grow in three seasons at East End Park, where he also enjoyed his first taste of European football in the Fairs Cup.

> What happened to me on the field at Ibrox that day can only come under the category of miracles. I scored a hat trick, the first player ever to do so against Rangers at Ibrox. A local boy, born and brought up within two hundred yards of the ground, scoring three goals to beat Rangers, the team he had supported all his life – it was just too crazy for words.

– SIR ALEX FERGUSON

FACTFILE

DUNFERMLINE ATHLETIC FOOTBALL CLUB
FOUNDED 1885
HOME: EAST END PARK, PERTH
CHAMPIONSHIPS: 2
SCOTTISH CUPS: 2

While playing for the Pars, Fergie endured his first genuinely heart-breaking moment in football, one which would teach him a valuable lesson for the managerial career which was already taking root in the back of his mind.

Dunfermline had qualified for the 1965 Scottish Cup final, beating Hibernian in the semi-final. Although he hadn't scored in the semi, he'd been instrumental and, as his team's top scorer for the season, he expected to be picked to play in the final.

The team for the final against Celtic wasn't announced until less than an hour before the game. When his name was not read out, Fergie blew his top.

"You bastard!" he shouted at Dunfermline manger Willie Cunningham, who was flanked by Chairman David Thomson and Secretary James McConville for what they clearly knew would be a delicate moment for their firebrand forward.

"I make no apology for the way I reacted," Ferguson still maintains. "My view is that when the manager is not prepared to give a dropped player his place by telling him the bad news in advance then there can be no complaint if, when the axe falls without warning fifty minutes before kick-off, there is an emotional response."

> **It is now my basic philosophy of management to deal personally with players who might have expected to be picked for a game but are not. I let them know the position before I announce the team in front of the squad.**
>
> **– SIR ALEX FERGUSON**

Dunfermline lost that Cup final 3–2 but, despite his disappointment, Alex Ferguson's place in the annals of Scottish football history was secure — he was the equal top scorer in the division for the 1965-66 season.

After another successful campaign in 1966-67, Ferguson was selected for an international tour with a Scottish League eleven (the closest he ever came to a genuine international cap). It was an eventful tour to Israel, Hong Kong, Australia, New Zealand and Canada.

The first stop in Tel Aviv just happened to coincide with the commencement of the Six Day War in June 1967. During the opening 'friendly' against the Israeli national team, Fergie hardly endeared himself to the home fans when he broke the nose of home favourite Mordecai Spiegler.

But that was nothing compared with what was to follow.

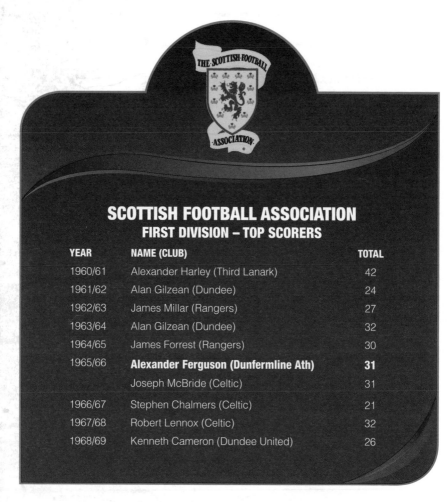

SCOTTISH FOOTBALL ASSOCIATION
FIRST DIVISION – TOP SCORERS

YEAR	NAME (CLUB)	TOTAL
1960/61	Alexander Harley (Third Lanark)	42
1961/62	Alan Gilzean (Dundee)	24
1962/63	James Millar (Rangers)	27
1963/64	Alan Gilzean (Dundee)	32
1964/65	James Forrest (Rangers)	30
1965/66	**Alexander Ferguson (Dunfermline Ath)**	**31**
	Joseph McBride (Celtic)	31
1966/67	Stephen Chalmers (Celtic)	21
1967/68	Robert Lennox (Celtic)	32
1968/69	Kenneth Cameron (Dundee United)	26

As the players enjoyed lunch in the holy city of Jerusalem on the eve of the second game, they heard fighter jets above and the sound of bombs exploding in the distance. It was the start of a deadly conflict which saw Israel batter Egyptian, Jordanian, Syrian and Iraqi troops along three of its borders with devastating success. It's probably fair to say that when you've been in that situation, a so-called 'war of words' with Arsene Wenger or Jose Mourinho is a piece of cake.

Things weren't a great deal better in Hong Kong for the second leg of the tour. The city was awash with armed soldiers as Maoist activists took to the streets. In part, the protest was directed at the touring capitalist boys from the West.

The rest of the trip was less eventful, although Ferguson — now considered one of Scotland's most dangerous strikers — was making headlines back home. He was being linked with a dream move to his beloved Rangers.

LOSING MY RELIGION

Politics, religion and football have always been inextricably linked in Scotland.

Apart from being enormous clubs with massive followings, Rangers and Celtic have traditionally been divided on religious grounds. To put it simply, Rangers is a Protestant club while Celtic has Irish Catholic origins.

Alex Ferguson is the product of a Protestant father and a Catholic mother. He was raised a Protestant, although he and his family have always been far more fanatical about football than religion. It's a similar story with Cathy, who could not be described as overly-devout in her Catholicism.

Prior to the world tour with Scotland, Ferguson had put in a transfer request at Dunfermline. In his absence, Rangers had prepared a £65,000 bid for his services, which was a record for deals between the two clubs at that time.

Within 24 hours of his return to Britain, the deal was done. In 1967, at the peak of his powers, he had realised a dream: he was officially a Rangers player.

But that dream would become a nightmare which still haunts him today.

> **On the day I signed for the club one of the directors, Ian McLaren, asked me about Cathy's religion. He wanted to know where we had been married. After I told him it was in the Registry Office he said 'well, that's all right then'.**
>
> **– SIR ALEX FERGUSON**

His debut season at Ibrox was an unqualified success. He finished as Rangers' top scorer and had quickly become a firm favourite among the fans. But, for the second successive season, Gers finished runners-up to Celtic in the League. The Hoops were on their way to a record-breaking run of nine successive titles under the great Jock Stein. Consequently, it was a turbulent period in Rangers' history.

By the end of Ferguson's second season at Rangers, Scot Symon — the manager who brought him to the club — had been sacked and "gossip about Cathy's religion was swirling around Ibrox". In his autobiography, Ferguson blames Rangers' PR manager Willie Allison for the gossip-mongering. He claims Allison insinuated that his first son, Mark, had been christened in a Catholic church, which was untrue.

Without warning, Ferguson found himself on the outer and down the pecking order in Rangers' striking department. He earned a recall to the first team for the 1969 Scottish Cup final against Celtic. However, he was ordered to man-mark the Bhoys' dangerous goal sneak Billy McNeill at corners. McNeill scored the first of Celtic's four unanswered goals after just two minutes in what turned out to be a disastrous final for Rangers.

Management desperately needed a scapegoat... and Fergie was it.

By the following pre-season, he was *persona non grata*, banished from the senior team.

Things quickly degenerated to the point where he was forced to train with the club's apprentices and was relegated to Rangers' third eleven, much to his — and the fans' — dismay. The situation also put an end to any international ambitions he may have harboured.

Rangers tried to offload Ferguson to Nottingham Forrest early in the 1969-70 season but, just as he was about to sign on the dotted line with the English club, he received an offer from his old boss at Dunfermline, Willie Cunningham, who was now managing Falkirk.

Once again, England would have to wait for Alex Ferguson.

It was with a heavy heart that he finally agreed to leave the club he'd adored his entire life. He blamed "religious bigotry of the deepest dye" for his untimely and premature demise at Ibrox.

> ## My hopes and ambitions were buried alive.
>
> **– SIR ALEX FERGUSON**

"No other experience in nearly forty years as a professional player and manager has created a scar as comparable with that left by the treatment I received at Ibrox," he lamented.

HOPES
AND
AMBITIONS

Ferguson spent the next three and a half seasons at Brockville Park, home of Falkirk FC. Like so many players before him, a career which once showed enormous promise — including the potential of playing for his country — had begun to peter out.

However, it was while injured at Falkirk that an opportunity appeared, seemingly out of nowhere. In fact, it may be no exaggeration to say that the knee injury he suffered in 1972 may have changed the course of football history.

Not only was he unable to accept an offer to join Hibernian, he began his first foray into the world of coaching. It began with a simple assignment to study Falkirk's future opponents for manager Willie Cunningham. While at Dunfermline, he'd earned his preliminary coaching badge and, later, undergone a two-week Scottish Football Association manager's course.

During his injury layoff, he was appointed first team coach at Falkirk and, at the end of his penultimate season at Brockville Park, he hit the books once again to add to his managerial qualifications.

After Cunningham was replaced as Falkirk manager, Ferguson was relieved of his coaching duties, which put him offside with new boss John Prentice. Seeking a gentle transition into retirement, he moved to Second Division Ayr United.

FACTFILE

AYR UNITED FOOTBALL CLUB
FOUNDED 1910
HOME: SOMERSET PARK
CHAMPIONSHIPS: 0
SCOTTISH CUPS: 0

After a single season at Somerset Park, Alex Ferguson finally pulled the pin on his playing career at the age of just 32, having been diagnosed with a relatively minor cardiac problem (which has never been a bother to him since).

There was no testimonial match, no drawn-out tribute and no public stroll down memory lane. The prospect of a life in management loomed large as he ran out for his final match against East Fife.

> In my case it was not really an ending but a beginning.
> – SIR ALEX FERGUSON

JUST HOW RED IS SIR ALEX FERGUSON?

He may have been a right-footed striker in his playing days but, when it comes to politics, Sir Alex is more left wing than centre forward.

He's no Karl Marx, but he had his family worried for a while there.

Throughout his youth, Fergie was the favourite grandchild of his paternal grandmother in Govan. In her eyes, little Alex could do no wrong. Well, almost.

Dear old Granny Irwin once gave him a frightful dressing-down he'll never forget. It was real 'hair dryer' stuff.

It was over politics, of all things. She discovered he'd become a trade union shop steward at the Remington factory after he'd joined his colleagues in a two-month strike to win better wages for apprentices.

"She (Grandma Irwin) went right through me. She said 'you're mother thinks you're a communist', pointing her finger at me," Sir Alex recalled.

"She prays every night you're not a communist."

"You'd better bloody not be. I'm telling you. I'd never forgive you."

Eventually he calmed her down and assured his Gran he most certainly was *not* a communist.

Since then, though, he's never been shy about offering a political opinion.

In his autobiography, he slammed the Conservative government for the state of the public hospital where his mother died in 1986.

"I have never ceased to curse the Tory government for vandalising the National Health Service. Margaret Thatcher's aggressive efforts to privatise health care in this country were a betrayal of a service that has been one of the proudest achievements of our society."

In 1998 he was 'outed' as a major political donor for the Labour Party and spoke openly in support of Gordon Brown ahead of the 2010 General Election.

"My loyalty to Labour is a part of who I am because I know what they do for people. Ever since it was founded, Labour has fought for ordinary working people and it does that just as much today," he told the *Mirror* on April 28, 2010.

In August 2010 he spoke at the funeral of Scottish trade union leader Jimmy Reid who, for a time, actually was a communist.

So, while he might wear red on the training pitch, Comrade Ferguson is definitely no pinko.

How to be Ferocious like Fergie:

- Football might be the ultimate example of mixing business with pleasure… but avoid mixing religion with football. They've always been ugly bedfellows. These days, of course, Fergie's Protestant upbringing doesn't matter a fig, although he does say "Jesus Christ" a lot when he's yelling at referees.

- Similarly, make a choice: you're either a politician or a manager. If you're a manager, voicing political opinions will only attract ridicule. And, if you really are a communist, go and manage China — the Premier League is awash with capitalist pigs.

- If you get bitten, bite back harder. But don't bite off more than you can chew. For instance, if you find yourself in a war zone, get the hell out of there. A big, hairy defender on a football pitch is nothing compared to bombs dropping from planes.

MY WAY OR THE HIGHWAY

" I'm a terrible loser. Speak to someone who played with me and I think you will find that I was a bad loser then.
— SIR ALEX FERGUSON

" He definitely is the world's worst loser. He hates getting beat at snooker. I've seen men transferred for beating him at snooker.
— GORDON STRACHAN

" Become a fan if you think Sir Alex Ferguson is a bad loser. Join the 'Sir Alex Ferguson is a sore loser' page!
— FACEBOOK, 2010

" I was scared to death of him the first time I met him. I still am.
— PAUL SCHOLES

" I needed two stitches after Alex kicked the boot at me.
— DAVID BECKHAM

In an age where political correctness rides roughshod over freedom of expression, Sir Alex Ferguson is a dinosaur. In his world, you make your own luck. Nothing comes without hard graft. And if you screw up, there's only one person to blame.

When Sir Alex Ferguson is your manager you have two choices. You can...

    (a) Do it his way.

or

    (b) Bugger off and play somewhere else.

> That is what a loser looks like. If you want to play for a bunch of losers then you can all fuck off to Highbury.
> **– SIR ALEX FERGUSON**
> (during a game against Arsenal in 2003)

Alex Ferguson first plonked his backside into the managerial hot seat during the summer of 1974 with second division strugglers East Stirlingshire. He made an instant impression.

"He terrified us. I'd never been afraid of anyone before but he was such a frightening bastard from the start. Everything was focused towards his goals. He always joined in with us in training and would have us playing in the dark until his five-a-side team won. He was ferocious, elbowing and kicking," East Stirlingshire forward Bobby McCulley told *The Guardian*.

Ferguson says he only took the job at East Stirlingshire (which at the time had only eight players on its books) because he'd performed badly during a job interview for a vacancy at his old club, Queens Park.

Conversely, he immediately warmed to the chairman of East Stirlingshire, Willie Muirhead, during his interview at Firs Park.

"The honesty in his face and the ease I felt in his company persuaded me to take a chance. Once he revealed the poverty of the playing resources, the decision began to look suicidal," he recalls.

Ferguson only managed 'The Shire' for three and a half months. For a club which had been around for almost a century, 'the Ferguson era' is still regarded as something of a golden period. (I guess when you win nothing, ever, it must just be nice to get your name in the paper now and then.)

In that time he'd scrambled together enough players to put out a competitive team, set up a youth system and delivered something the club had been sorely missing over the previous few seasons — wins.

> "The highlight of Ferguson's time in charge was The Shire's first home League win over Falkirk in 70 years, on 5 October 1974. Ferguson played mind games, telling his players the local paper favoured Falkirk, and booking a pre-match meal at the hotel Falkirk always used. He ordered his players to laugh and joke within sight of the Falkirk players to give the impression his was a team in great spirits. It had the desired effect and The Shire won 2–0.
> – eaststirlingshirefc.co.uk

In October 1974 Ferguson was invited to a secret meeting with his old mate Willie Cunningham, who was then managing St Mirren. Cunningham was retiring from football and urged Fergie to consider applying for the job at Love Street. He was tempted. St Mirren was a club with big support, financial stability and great potential. But his loyalty to East Stirlingshire put him off applying. He turned to a legend for advice.

"I phoned Jock Stein at Celtic Park."

The great man's advice was simple.

"Go and sit in the stand at Love Street and look around, then do the same at Firs Park and you will get your answer. All the best."

A few days later Ferguson signed for St Mirren. But it was with "a dull sense of failure" rather than excitement for the challenge ahead that Fergie walked away from tiny East Stirlingshire, the club which gave him his first chance as a manager.

One of the most common criticisms of Sir Alex Ferguson is that he's old-fashioned. He's not really... he's just set in his ways. He's used his favourite training drills for three decades and believes that repetition and relentless application are the only ways to bring consistent success.

But suggestions that Fergie's something of a football Luddite could not be further from the truth. When it comes to keeping players physically fit and mentally fresh, or bringing them back from injury, he is an innovator. He was the first manager to hire a full-time dietician, whom he brings to all far-flung destinations. (It's a nightmare finding decent haggis in Barcelona these days.)

While he listens to the science, he also relies on his gut. You can strap heart-rate monitors to players, measure how far they run during a match, how much weight they lose and how much fluid they ingest. You can monitor their diet, sleep patterns, toilet habits and sex life... but if they miss a shot from two yards out, all the science in the world won't get you three points.

He believes the only way to achieve lasting success is to have a thriving youth system. And that means hiring scouts — dozens of them. That was the key to his success at St Mirren.

> Sometimes I feel that I have known nearly as many scouts as (Robert) Baden-Powell.
>
> **– SIR ALEX FERGUSON**

Through his incredible network of friends, former coaches, teammates and confidantes Ferguson scraped together a motley bunch of youngsters who, within three seasons, had propelled the unfashionable Saints to the top of the First Division (Scotland's second tier in 1976-77).

He and his team brought in players who would become legends at Love Street: Tony Fitzpatrick, John McDonald, Billy Stark, Bobbie Reid, Frank McGarvey and Joe Miller.

With an average age of just 19, these players would form the backbone of Fergie's first title-winning team, albeit a lower division championship.

But if Fergie's rise at St Mirren was spectacular, his fall was equally breathtaking.

In the same season the club moved into the Premier Division, Ferguson fell out with Chairman Willie Todd. Fergie had secretly begun talks to take over as manager at Aberdeen, but Todd found out — and promptly sacked him. It remains the only time in his managerial career he's ever been fired.

> Willie Todd and I were no longer talking to each other and when Aberdeen made another approach to me there could be only one reaction.
>
> — SIR ALEX FERGUSON

> Four days before he eventually left I knew perfectly well that he had told all the staff that he was moving to Aberdeen. It was a clear breach of contract on his part. I had no option but to sack him in the end.
>
> — WILLIE TODD, CHAIRMAN, ST MIRREN

After all I'd done for them
(St Mirren) I felt degraded.
– SIR ALEX FERGUSON

The ugly post-script to the saga of the sacking is that a furious Fergie took St Mirren to an industrial tribunal — and lost. Although, as Ian Cruise of the *Mirror Football Blog* mused in 2009, "You can't help thinking St Mirren lost rather more though, can you?"

If moving from East Stirlingshire to St Mirren was a big step for a young manager, switching to Aberdeen was a proverbial giant leap.

When Ferguson arrived at Pittodrie in the middle of 1978, one of either Celtic or Rangers had claimed 67 of the 78 titles which had been won in the 20th century. By any measure, overcoming either of the Old Firm — let alone both — would be a monumental task. For their part, Aberdeen had won just one title in 76 attempts.

He put together a team which boasted the silky skills of a young Steve Archibald, the goal scoring prowess of Mark McGhee, the rugged defence of Doug Rougvie and a couple of Scottish legends who are still involved in football today: Gordon Strachan and Alex McLeish.

In 1979-80, the Dons managed the extraordinary feat of home and away victories over both Glasgow giants and were nipping at the heels of Celtic at the top of the table for the first half of the season. At the same time Sylvester Stallone was dominating cinema screens around the world with a reprise of his iconic Rocky Balboa character.

Aberdeen were riding with the punches against the heavyweights of the Scottish Premier Division and, surprisingly, staying on their feet. But no-one truly expected a *Rocky II* finish, with the underdog prevailing over the cocky, all-conquering champion.

Heavy snowfalls in January 1980 saw a number of matches postponed at chilly Pittodrie. Down south, Celtic were gaining momentum, extending their lead to 10 points at the top of the table, although Aberdeen had three games in hand.

Instead of stumbling in the final rounds, the Dons confounded their critics with a powerful combination of counter-punches. They beat Celtic twice in a pair of epic encounters and picked up points in all of their make-up matches.

The knock-out blow came when they smashed five goals past Hibs on the penultimate weekend of the season. The elusive title was finally theirs after 25 years. Apollo Creed had been counted out and 'Rocky' Ferguson had his first major title.

	1979–80 Scottish Premier Division table								
P	Team	Pld	W	D	L	GF	GA	GD	Pts
1	Aberdeen	36	19	10	7	68	36	32	**48**
2	Celtic	36	18	11	7	61	38	23	**47**
3	St. Mirren	36	15	12	9	56	49	7	**42**
4	Dundee United	36	12	13	11	43	30	13	**37**
5	Rangers	36	15	7	14	50	46	4	**37**
6	Morton	36	14	8	14	51	46	5	**36**
7	Partick Thistle	36	11	14	11	43	47	-4	**36**
8	Kilmarnock	36	11	11	14	36	52	-16	**33**
9	Dundee	36	10	6	20	47	73	-26	**26**
10	Hibernian	36	6	6	24	29	67	-38	**18**

As you'd expect, Celtic hit back hard in 1980-81, with Aberdeen finishing second and Rangers third. It was a similar story in 1981-82, although Fergie lifted the Scottish Cup for the first time with a 4—1 hammering of Rangers at Hampden, having knocked out Celtic in the fourth round. It was a consolation prize after two years of fruitless hard work in the league, but it would have far-reaching consequences a year later.

1982-83 would catapult Alex Ferguson into the managerial stratosphere and forever link the unfashionable city of Aberdeen with the pristine sweetness of Gothenburg in Sweden. The Dons finished third in the Premier Division that season, equal on points with Celtic, but the dip in their league form can be partly explained by their incredible European adventure.

The club had never tasted European success of any kind, but went into the Cup Winners Cup competition full of confidence after five seasons holding their own in what was now being called the 'New Firm', a term which gave the Aberdeen equal standing with Celtic and Rangers in the football lexicon — a miracle in itself.

Ferguson's men massacred Swiss side FC Sion 11—1 over two legs in the qualifying round of the tournament and struggled to a narrow 1—0/0—0 victory over Albanians Dinamo Tirana in the first round. They comfortably accounted for Polish team Lech Poznan 2—0/1—0 in the second round and found themselves in the quarter finals against German giants Bayern Munich.

Fergie and his assistant Archie Knox took turns travelling to Germany to prepare for the first leg and were rewarded with a crucial nil-all draw at Munich's Olympiastadion. In the return leg at a sold-out Pittodrie Stadium, Aberdeen twice went behind and faced almost certain heartbreak before the boss made three vital substitutions.

Cue the *Rocky* theme music.

Following Neil Simpson's goal just before the break, McLeish made it 2—2, scoring after a rehearsed mix-up between Strachan and John McMaster. Still facing elimination on the away goals rule, substitute John Hewitt sent the stadium — and the city — into a frenzy, knocking in the winner after the German keeper could only parry a shot from Eric Black.

Against all odds, little Aberdeen had knocked out one of the world's great football powerhouses and were into the semi finals of the Cup Winners Cup.

After the drama of the tie against the Germans, the semis were an anti-climax. They dismissed Belgian club Waterschei (who?) 5—2 over two legs. Out of nowhere, Aberdeen were into a major European final. Awaiting the Dons in Gothenburg were none other than Real Madrid, six-time European Cup champions and, perhaps, the scariest football club in the world.

The Scottish scramble across the North Sea was unprecedented — 14,000 fans made the trip any way they could. The only thing more elusive than a match ticket was a place on the St Clair ferry.

Eric Black gave Aberdeen an early lead after just seven minutes from a set piece, only to see Juanito equalise on 14 minutes following a diabolical back pass from McLeish.

But the Dons were rampant. The match highlights reveal wave after wave of Aberdeen attacks down the left wing, with Peter Weir terrorising the Spaniards. They just couldn't land the killer blow. So, in driving rain and with the score locked at 1—1, the game went into extra time.

The Scottish onslaught continued until, with just eight minutes left on the clock, little John Hewitt popped up again and headed himself — and Aberdeen — into the history books with the winning goal.

"I was watching Hewitt, who was making his way into their box in a straight line, with no thought of bending his run as he had been constantly told he should. As McGhee crossed, I was muttering all sorts of abuse of Hewitt. So, of course, the ball landed on his head and he won the Cup for us," Ferguson would later write.

Aberdeen erupted. Apart from the pubs, the entire district had shut down during the two hours of the game. After the match residents, young and old, streamed from their homes and into the city centre for the party to end all parties.

> His work at Aberdeen was stunning. He broke the monopoly of the Old Firm of Rangers and Celtic, won the Scottish title and landed the European Cup Winners Cup. Ferguson, fiercely abrasive, fanatical in protecting his club's interests was, above all, a winner.
>
> — JAMES LAWTON, *THE INDEPENDENT*

Half a million people lined the streets of Aberdeen to welcome home the heroes of Gothenburg, 1983. It was — and perhaps always will be — the proudest moment in the club's history. Ferguson was hailed as a genius and a managerial legend was born.

In his next season, riding a wave of invincibility, Fergie led the Dons to a League and Cup double. They beat Hamburg SV to collect the European Super Cup but lost to Porto in the semi finals of the tournament they'd won so handsomely a year earlier. They made it back-to-back Scottish titles in 1984-85 but squandered the chance to make history and win a fourth straight Scottish Cup, losing to Dundee United in a semi final replay.

The death of his idol Jock Stein in late 1985 was a hammer blow for Ferguson, and appeared to be a turning point in his life. He'd been assisting the legendary manager at Scotland's World Cup qualifier against Wales in Cardiff when Stein collapsed and died immediately after the game. Ferguson had to break the news to Jock's family.

"It was as if the king had died. In football terms, the king *had* died," he said.

By this time, Ferguson was a manager in demand. There had been offers from Rangers, Arsenal, Wolverhampton and Tottenham. It was clearly just a matter of time before he'd move on to bigger things. At the end of the season he confessed to Aberdeen Chairman Dick Donald that he was ready for a new challenge.

> He shook me slightly when said categorically that there was only one job I should consider preferable to the one I held at Aberdeen. Asked to name the club, he said, 'Manchester United. If you really want a challenge – that is the biggest in football'.
>
> **– SIR ALEX FERGUSON**

After a disappointing fourth place in the 1985-86 season, Aberdeen compensated with a Cups double: the Scottish Cup (Ferguson's fourth) and the Scottish League Cup, which had previously eluded him.

There had been enormous speculation linking him to the Manchester United job in the summer of 1986, but he claimed there was no contact with the Red Devils until months later. Yet as the 1986-87 season took shape down the M6 in England, it was clear that Ron Atkinson's grip on the manager's job at Old Trafford was slipping.

On 5 November, 1986, Ferguson received a phone call from United director Mike Edelsen, who put him through to Chairman Martin Edwards. Within hours they had met face-to-face, agreed terms and shaken hands on a deal for Fergie to replace Atkinson with immediate effect. It was as simple as that — no courting, no huge salary (he earned less in his first season at Old Trafford than he did in his last at Pittodrie) and no need to go away and think about it. His answer was "yes, yes, yes".

Manchester United — the biggest club in the world — had

their man. And Alex Ferguson had been given the kind of opportunity he'd coveted his whole life.

Where better to chase a rainbow than Old Trafford, the *Theatre Of Dreams?*

Sir Alex Ferguson – 1974 v 2004
A tale of two wish lists

Sir Alex Ferguson says every season is a learning experience.

Just keeping up with changes to the game – and the business of the game – can be exhausting… not to mention expensive.

While football has been about money for much longer than most sporting romantics would care to admit, the following table is a stark reminder of how the enormous pressure of managing the most popular football club in the world also has its rewards, in terms of financial backing.

Here's a snapshot of two separate seasons in Fergie's life as a manager. The difference: exactly 30 years. (And a truck-load of "bread 'n' honey".)

What makes this comparison even more extraordinary is that the figures from 1974 are only sign-on fees. All his signings back then were free transfers – the club was broke and couldn't afford transfer fees.

1974 EAST STIRLINGSHIRE	2004 MANCHESTER UNITED
Tom Gourlay (Partick) £750	Louis Saha (Fulham) £12,850,000 [Summer]
Billy Hulston (Clyde) £900	Alan Smith (Leeds) £7,050,000)
Jimmy Mullen (Partick) £150	Gabriel Heinze (PSG) £6,900,000
George Adams (Partick) £150	Wayne Rooney (Everton) £30,000,000
TOTAL 1974: £1,950	2004: £56,800,000

HAIR DRYERS AND FLYING TEA CUPS

> **"** He would stand nose-to-nose with you and just shout and bawl, and you would end up with your hair behind your head. **"**
>
> **— MARK HUGHES**

Sir Alex Ferguson's tongue is as deadly as a Mike Tyson left hook.

In fact, it's no exaggeration to say the fiery Scot is as famous for his temper as he is for his extraordinary success as a manager. On a good day, a steely stare from Fergie is enough to strike fear into the heart of even the burliest of footballers. On a bad day, he can erupt like Krakatoa.

Mark Hughes was the one who famously put a name to the vein-popping tirades which have become such a hallmark of Ferguson's leadership — he labelled it the *hair dryer treatment* — and it's now part of football folk lore.

"The hair dryer thing was started by Sparky (Hughes) — he owned up to it after he left. I can understand that because of my policy in the dressing room."

A newspaper once claimed Fergie used to sneak off behind the grandstand at East Stirlingshire to practice screaming at his players. It's a good story, but he denies it.

He insists there's nothing contrived about his volcanic eruptions. They come from the pit of his stomach. They come from his father. They come from being Scottish. And they come without warning.

These days he claims to have mellowed, describing himself as "a pussycat". But dozens of players, rival managers, referees and journalists would disagree.

"When somebody challenges me in there, I have to go for them. I believe you cannot avoid confrontation. I had a bust-up with Schmikes (giant Danish goalkeeper Peter Schmeichel) once. He was towering over me and the other players were almost covering their eyes. We're eye-to-eye and I'm looking up and thinking to myself, 'if he does hit me, I know I'm dead'."

Although he's famously unrepentant, Fergie once confessed to seriously worrying about having such a short fuse.

At St Mirren he once threw and smashed a Coke bottle over the heads of his players as he roared at them after a match... which, incidentally, they'd won 1—0. Imagine if they'd lost!

One afternoon at Aberdeen he hit a tea urn so hard while giving Gordon Strachan the half-time hair dryer treatment that he nearly broke his hand. That, in turn, made him so angry he hurled a tray of (full) tea cups at his players.

Then, of course, there was the infamous Beckham boot in the eye.

In February 2003 Manchester United crashed out of the FA Cup at the hands of arch-rivals Arsenal. Fergie stormed into the dressing room after the 2—0 defeat in a foul temper.

As the hair dryer was switched to top gear, he kicked a boot which was lying in front of him. It flew up and hit David Beckham in the face. Becks needed two stitches to a cut above his left eye and the tabloids had a field day. "Scarface!", "Beckham gets the boot", they roared. Ferguson apologised, describing the incident as a freak accident.

"If I tried it a hundred or a million times it couldn't happen again. If I could I would have carried on playing."

Seven years later, in typical understated fashion, Beckham simply described his old boss as "a scary man".

How to be Ferocious like Fergie:

⬎ Being the world's worst loser is nothing — everyone gets upset when their team is beaten. But to be seriously ferocious, be a bad winner. Choose precisely the greatest moment in the history of your football club, when thousands of fans are deliriously happy, to show what a truly grouchy bastard you are.

⬎ When you have an accent which half of your players can't understand, pump up the volume. If your message isn't getting through at 10 decibels, try it again at 100 decibels. For added spice, start every second word with F, toss a tea cup and let the spittle fly freely. They'll get the idea.

⬎ If you're going to smash and throw things, avoid glass or heavy items which can break bones (especially yours) or pierce skin. If there's nothing to throw or punch and you fancy lashing out with your foot, make sure the prettiest metrosexual footballer ever born isn't in your immediate firing line.

Being the world's
worst loser is nothing
– everyone gets upset
when their team is
beaten. But to be
seriously ferocious,
↘**BE A BAD
WINNER.**

ON THE WAGON

When it comes to alcohol, Sir Alex Ferguson is a genius... or a hypocrite. One or the other!

When his players get mixed up with booze, he carries on like it's like the end of the world. He says the most important aspect to his resurrecting of Manchester United was conquering the drinking culture at the club. And, at times, his anti-alcohol mantra has had a frightening — almost religious — zeal to it.

But take a close look at Fergie's nose and cheeks. He's no teetotaller — that's the face of a drinker. He adores wine. He's a genuine connoisseur, too, making regular trips to the vineyards of France to load up on top quality (and often very, very expensive) plonk. He's even talked about buying his own vineyard when — or if — he ever retires from football.

Despite the hard line he takes with his players, he has confessed to his own alcohol-fuelled benders in his playing days — although, to be fair, they were few and far between.

It's easy, of course, to suggest a double-standard. But, obviously, a manager who's well past retirement age doesn't need to keep in shape like a footballer who plays every weekend. And, of course, men in their seventies drink alcohol in a totally different way to boys in their twenties. Well, most do.

Maybe Fergie's attitude to booze is cosmic. He was, after all, born on New Year's Eve — and anyone who's experienced Hogmanay in Scotland will know that behind all the Pagan prancing, it's just a good excuse for a nation-wide piss up.

"Our clubs and their managers have frequently shown a weak-kneed reluctance to deal with the menace of boozing.
– SIR ALEX FERGUSON

When Fergie walked into Old Trafford in November 1986, he felt too many of the players were drinking too much, too often.

At the very moment he was putting pen to paper on his first contract at United, his future players were on a drinking binge to farewell his predecessor, Ron Atkinson. It was a Thursday night and the team had a match on Saturday. Ferguson quickly realised his first meeting with the squad would be a confrontation over booze.

He delayed the showdown until after his first game in charge (it would have been hard to rip into the squad if they'd won 6—0). They lost 2—0 to lowly Oxford. He let them have it with both barrels.

Fergie wasn't only concerned with players' fitness levels — he felt many were lightweights who couldn't compete physically and were prone to injury. He also feared for the reputation of the club and the value of the United brand. He imposed an immediate drinking ban for any player in training... which was immediately ignored by several players.

Whenever Fergie is called upon to name the best players he's ever coached, Bryan Robson is always near the top of the list. ("He was a miracle of commitment, a human marvel.") But when the new manager arrived at Old Trafford, Robson — the club captain — found himself on another list: the Gaffer's drinking hit-list.

He singled out Robson, Paul McGrath and Norman Whiteside. He succeeded in convincing 'Captain Marvel' to cut down, although Robson refused to give up drinking all together and would often argue the point with the manager.

But Ferguson couldn't get through to Whiteside or McGrath, no matter how hard he tried.

Fergie: "The worst binges usually occurred when McGrath and Whiteside took to the bars as a double act. I was saddened as well as infuriated by the way they abused themselves, since both had the sort of talent given to only a tiny elite of footballers."

It came to a head when the two went out drinking in the week leading up to an FA Cup tie in 1989. They went on an "epic bender" on the Tuesday before the game. Fergie blasted them and fined them the maximum allowable under PFA rules. The very next night they were painting the town red again.

"Next morning on the training pitch, McGrath could hardly jog properly. He was obviously the worst for wear," Ferguson says.

While Whiteside would listen politely as his boss gently (or, Fergie being Fergie, not-so-gently) pointed out the dangers drinking posed to his career, he never really changed his habits beyond the occasional week or two of abstinence.

He delayed the showdown until after his first game in charge. They lost 2–0 to lowly Oxford. He let them have it with

↘**BOTH BARRELS.**

> I always felt in control. If you're eighteen or nineteen, playing for the best club in the world, getting reasonably well paid, you are entitled to go and have a few beers. I never thought it was harming my football.
>
> **— NORMAN WHITESIDE**

McGrath was an altogether different beast. Ferguson felt that when he spoke to him all the hair dryer treatment in the world would go in one ear out and out the other.

He even enlisted revered club legend Sir Matt Busby to have a quiet word to the wayward star. When that failed, he brought in his local priest — again to no avail. God was Fergie's last resort; at the end of the season McGrath was shipped off to Aston Villa for £400,000.

Much later, it was revealed that McGrath's problem was far more serious than a young man having a good time. Alcohol didn't just ruin his career — it severely damaged his life.

In an interview with the *Daily Mail* in February 2010 he said, "I hadn't tasted drink until I was 18. The minute I did, I felt comfortable."

"I wasn't in the First Division of drinkers back then. No way. I was fit, young and able to train."

"The problem was that myself and Norman Whiteside would be injured for such a length of time. We'd be in the gym or in the treatment room watching the other lads play and for us it was a case of, 'what shall we be doing this afternoon?' Obviously, we could have been laid up in bed recuperating. But we would sort of look at each other and the conversation would develop along the lines of, 'no, we can't. We can't. We can't, can we? Ah, go on. Let's go for one or two.' Eventually, we would be sat there all afternoon, drinking."

"I don't cringe now at the thought that I went on to the pitch sometimes having had a few drinks. Believe it or not, having those drinks helped me," McGrath says.

> **I ran round the pitch trying to hold my breath on occasions. Mainly because the person I was up against would know that I'd had a drink and I didn't want them to.**
>
> **– PAUL McGRATH**

Lee Sharpe was another United youngster who enjoyed the alcohol-fuelled social scene of Manchester's notorious nightclubs in the 1990s.

"I was still going out with my mates, usually with a flock of girls chirruping around us, me at the centre grinning, talking, dancing, flirting, so it all made sense."

In his autobiography, *My Idea Of Fun*, Sharpe mocked Ferguson's assault on the drinking culture at Old Trafford.

"In an ideal world, Alex Ferguson would have preferred if his players didn't drink at all, spent their days off playing golf and were always tucked up in bed at 9.45 having watched a few training videos," he wrote.

Sharpe clashed with Ferguson towards the end of the 1991-92 season after a run of four games in six days, with a match against Liverpool scheduled to make it five in ten days. Following a defeat to West Ham at Upton Park, just four days before the trip to Anfield, Fergie discovered Sharpe had been on the tiles in Blackpool two nights earlier with the angelic Welsh youngster Ryan Giggs. Fuming, he drove straight to Sharpe's house.

Music was blasting out from the house. When the door was opened to me, I burst in with all guns blazing. There was a full-scale party going on.

I went berserk. I ordered everybody out of the house and as each apprentice passed I gave him a cuff on the back of the head.

– SIR ALEX FERGUSON

It took Ferguson more than five years to weed out the trouble-makers and change the drinking culture at Old Trafford.

It's no coincidence that United's ascent of the league table, to the point where Ferguson's team could launch a genuine title bid, bore a direct correlation to the decline in the drinking culture.

By Fergie's own admission, it was success in Cup competitions which bought him time to build a squad which could achieve his dream for long-lasting success. Without those early trophies, his career at Old Trafford would have been significantly shorter.

The 1990 FA Cup was the first major trophy Alex Ferguson won in England. It came three and a half years after his arrival at the club. You can be sure that these days few of the giant clubs in England or on the continent would give a manager that sort of time to put together a winning team (let alone the additional three years it took him to land the big one, the Premier League crown).

Victory against Crystal Palace in that Cup final was the beginning an extraordinary era for Manchester United. Defeat, however, might have stopped Fergie in his tracks. After a 3—3 draw at Wembley, United won the replay 1—0. His joy was tarnished by the controversy surrounding the decision to drop the man who'd kept goal for most of his managerial career, Jim Leighton, in favour of Les Sealey.

"The headlines the next morning were varied, with the most severe accusing me of betraying Leighton. If we had lost the Cup final and I had lost my job, would Jim Leighton have felt guilty? To put it bluntly, I believe Jim was selfish," Fergie says.

On his way to victory in the 1991 UEFA Cup Winners Cup final, Fergie had cause to visit the south of France to scout United's quarterfinal opponents, Montpellier. It was there, while staying in the hotel of wine enthusiast Jean Phillippe Casalta, that Fergie's interest in grapes was uncorked.

United beat Barcelona 2—1 in the final in Rotterdam, three weeks after losing the League Cup final against Sheffield Wednesday. Six months later they took on Red Star Belgrade in the European Super Cup final and triumphed 1—0. The next trophy was the 1991-92 League Cup which bought Fergie yet more time following a League campaign which saw them overtaken at the final hurdle by eventual champions Leeds United. They were getting closer.

English Football Association 1991-92 First Division table									
Pos	Team	Pld	W	D	L	GF	GA	GD	Pts
1	Leeds United	42	13	8	0	38	13	+37	82
2	Manchester United	42	12	7	2	34	13	+30	78
3	Sheffield Wednesday	42	13	5	3	39	24	+13	75
4	Arsenal	42	12	7	2	51	23	+34	72

The next season began with much fanfare as the sparkling new 'Premier League' was launched.

The League was flush with cash from a television deal which had seen TV revenues jump from £6.3 million for two years in 1986 to £304 million for five years in 1992. (By 2010, the global television rights were worth more than £1.7 billion per season.)

There was never a better time to kick off a period of unprecedented world domination.

BOTTLING IT

Sir Alex Ferguson's hard-nosed approach to alcohol dates way back to 1963 when he was struggling to get a game at St Johnstone.

He'd suffered a horrifying injury which had left him with a shattered cheekbone, a broken nose and a fracture in the bone above his eye. Fergie returned to the team for a reserves game against Celtic.

The Saints were hammered 10—1 and lost 11—2 in their next game against the Kilmarnock reserves. Fergie felt his career was "grinding to a halt" and even contemplated migrating to Canada.

"If you want to make it as a player, you have to be fully committed and willing to make sacrifices — and in both respects I was coming up short," he confessed.

"I had begun to enjoy myself overmuch socially and a terrible bust-up was inevitable when Dad smelled drink on me one Saturday night."

Not surprisingly, Alex Ferguson Senior hit the roof and, not for the first time, father and son found themselves no longer on speaking terms.

What followed was a transformation of gargantuan proportions, highlighted with that fortuitous promotion to the senior team and the extraordinary hat-trick against Rangers which changed his life.

A few years later Fergie had another brush with the bottle which, he now admits, was not his finest hour. It was on a pre-season tour of Denmark after his first season with Rangers.

A newspaper article had appeared back home with a headline along the lines of "Ferguson finished at Ibrox". When manager Dave White hinted that the club's PR officer Willie Allison (whom Fergie felt was undermining him on the basis of his wife's religion) was responsible for the leak, Ferguson was furious.

"Although I was not a drinker, I was in the mood to make an exception that afternoon. (Teammates) John Greig and Alex Smith were also in the company and we sat in the bar for hours, more than long enough for me to be well gone."

When the group returned to the team hotel, a drunken Fergie delivered what might have been his first ever hair dryer treatment, verbally attacking Allison, but was bundled off by his mates before too much damage had been done. After calm was restored and Fergie had been put to bed, his Royal Fieriness awoke and roared downstairs in his pyjamas for another crack at Allison. Again, his teammates had to drag him away.

He was given a meal of steak and chips (and a glass of milk) but, in his infinite wisdom, decided to join his teammates in a "whole night clubbing in Copenhagen".

A little-known fact about Alex Ferguson is that he once owned a pub — in fact, for a time, he had two. And they weren't exactly the classiest drinking establishments in old Glasgow town, either. He bought the licence for the Burns Cottage pub, in the docks district, during his final year as a player and promptly renamed it *Fergie's*.

Like a Scottish Basil Fawlty, he tried to attract a better class of clientele, but to no avail. Within weeks, there was an all-in brawl in the bar, leaving blood-soaked bodies scattered on the pavement outside. Fergie was warned by police that he could lose his licence if the carnage continued.

Unperturbed, he bought a share in another bar — called Shaws — which again turned into a nightmare. By the time he was managing St Mirren he decided enough was enough, and sold out of both pubs.

"I was sick of having to come home at weekends with a cut head or swollen jaw from trying to keep peace in the pub."

"I was sick of having to come home at weekends with a **↘CUT HEAD OR SWOLLEN JAW** from trying to keep peace in the pub."

SWIG WHEN YOU'RE WINNING

In his autobiography, *Managing My Life*, Fergie named the chapter about his arrival at Manchester United "Drinking To Failure".

But there were plenty of occasions when Fergie was drinking to success.

Like so many aspects of his management style, he used booze as part of his ritual mind games against opposition managers.

When Aberdeen made the European Cup Winners Cup final he took a sage piece of advice from his mentor, Jock Stein, which he's followed to this day.

"One interesting suggestion was that I should buy the Real Madrid manager, the great Alfredo Di Stefano, a gift of good whisky. 'Let him feel important' said Jock, 'as if you are thrilled just to be in the final and only there to make up the numbers'."

He pulled the same trick with Johan Cruyff ahead of United's showdown with Barcelona in the same competition in 1991.

His post-match drinking as a manager is now famous, largely for the company he keeps.

He complained to Jose Mourinho that the wine he offered after a match against Chelsea at Stamford Bridge in 2005 was poor, prompting 'the Special One' to splash out £250 on a bottle for the return fixture at Old Trafford.

While managing Burnley in 2009, Owen Coyle dispatched his PR Manager to buy two bottles of the best red wine money could buy, ahead of the aptly-named Clarets' surprise win over the champions at Turf Moor. Knowing nothing about wine, teetotaller Coyle put the bottles in the refrigerator. Fortunately, his faux pas was picked up by a vigilant staffer. (He should never have mentioned it at the press conference afterwards.)

If there's one man Fergie would like to drink with, it's Arsene Wenger, the Arsenal manager, but the Frenchman refuses to socialise with him.

"As it happens, Arsene Wenger is somebody I would like to get to know better. People who do know him well tell me he is a good man. But I don't suppose I'll ever find that out for myself. He seems to pull down the shutters when you meet up with him and never has a drink with you after a game."

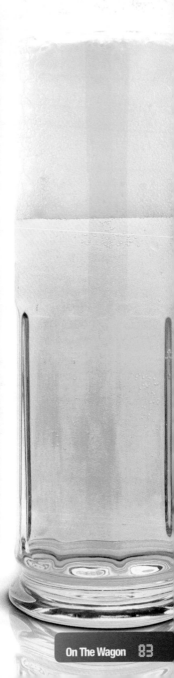

KEEPING IT IN
THE FAMILY

Football may have denied Sir Alex Ferguson the opportunity to be the perfect father and husband, but he's always fiercely defended his family.

He was accused of nepotism when he signed his son during his early days at Manchester United. Darren Ferguson made 27 first team appearances for the Red Devils, including 15 in their 1992-93 title-wining campaign, which was enough to earn him a winner's medal. But, after leaving United, he never played top division football again, spending a number of seasons at Wolverhampton and Wrexham.

When Darren moved into management, he benefited more than once from loan signings from his old man. At Preston North End he 'borrowed' Danny Wellbeck and Matthew James, while earlier — at Peterborough — he was loaned young defender James Chester.

Darren's twin, Jason, played some reserves football at Aberdeen but, in his post-football career as a player's agent, he faced allegations of favouritism from his Dad. The accusations went way beyond nepotism.

A 2004 BBC documentary *Father and Son* alleged, among other things, that Jason had exploited his father's position to the benefit of himself and two agencies: L'Attitude, where he was employed, and Elite Sports, where he was a director.

Darren Ferguson

The programme questioned payments to the agencies relating to the transfers of Massimo Taibi and Jaap Stam. It also revealed that Elite represented 13 members of the United squad.

Sir Alex later accused the BBC of "breathtaking arrogance" and demanded an apology, which was not forthcoming.

"They did a story about my son that was a whole lot of nonsense. It was all made-up stuff and brown paper bags and all that kind of carry-on. It was a horrible attack on my son's honour and he should never have been accused of that. But it is such a huge organisation that they will never apologise."

In the aftermath, United made stringent changes to their policies involving player agents and Fergie declared he would never speak to the BBC again. So far, he's been true to his word.

And finally, on the subject of family, Fergie hasn't just looked after his sons. His brother Martin was, for a time, United's chief scout. He was criticised by fans for his involvement in the disastrous signings of Kleberson, Diego Forlan and Eric Djemba-Djemba. These days Martin Ferguson is no longer involved at Old Trafford.

How to be Ferocious like Fergie:

⬎ If you're planning on parading around hotel bars picking fights, get a decent pair of pyjamas. Nothing puts you off an evening G&T like a half-dressed, drunken Scotsman.

⬎ When you give a good-looking Brazilian teenager a hundred thousand quid a week, don't be surprised if goes off the rails occasionally and — heaven forbid — has a drink. You can ban your players from nightclubs during the season but, these days, when half the team live in fully-staffed mansions or castles, the nightclubs come to them. Youth and wealth will never be separated from sex, drugs and rock 'n' roll.

⬎ Don't drink the night before a big press conference. There are times when Fergie pops up on television looking like Rudolph the Red-nosed Reindeer.

There are times when Fergie pops up on television looking like **RUDOLPH** ⬎**THE RED-NOSED REINDEER.**

MORE SILVERWARE THAN
BUCKINGHAM PALACE

Sir Alex Ferguson and Eric Cantona are polar opposites. In fact, Fergie has more in common with a polar bear than he does with the brooding French actor-cum-footballer.

Yet, as sure as a toasted ham and cheese sarnie is the same as a croque monsieur, football's Odd Couple made magic together at Old Trafford, laying the foundations for a generation of dominance.

Their love story began in the final weeks of the 1991-92 season. Ferguson had come within a whisker of winning the prize he'd coveted more than any other, the English First Division title. After leading for a huge portion of the season the Red Devils lost three games in a row on the run-in and were overtaken by Leeds United.

Inexplicably, Manchester United had gone from averaging two goals per game in the first half of that season, to one in the second. Just as the battle with Leeds United came down to the wire, the goals dried up for the boys from the red half of Manchester.

So, it was back to the drawing board for the Ferocious One. Clearly, something had to change. In the summer of 1992 he was desperate to find that 'missing link'— a creative genius who could help United make the transition from being a good, possibly great, team... to champions.

At first, Ferguson was convinced Alan Shearer was his man.

21-year-old Shearer had netted 13 goals for lowly Southampton in 1991-92, earning himself a place in the England squad half way through the season.

Ferguson had been talking to Southampton manager Ian Branfoot for six months about Shearer. He'd reached an understanding that he wouldn't bother the club or the player until Shearer had returned from his summer tour with England.

So poor Fergie must have choked on his cornflakes when he read that Shearer had begun negotiating with Blackburn as soon as he was back in England. Rovers' manager Kenny Dalglish was splashing steel magnate Jack Walker's cash like he was an Emirati Sheik or a Russian oil oligarch.

Desperate, Fergie phoned Shearer direct.

> "Our talk did not last long. I found him very hard work and quite surly. One of the first things he said to me was 'why haven't you been interested in me before now? Kenny Dalglish was phoning me regularly'."
>
> **– SIR ALEX FERGUSON**

Shearer moved to Rovers for £3.6 million, with David Speedie going in the opposite direction. Fergie learned a valuable lesson about buying players in the new Premier League Promised Land.

An even higher priority for Ferguson, however, was Sheffield Wednesday's David Hurst, who'd played alongside Shearer with England a few months earlier. Ferguson contacted Wednesday manger Trevor Francis but was given the "short shrift". No deal.

So, United went into the 1992-93 season having signed just Dion Dublin from Cambridge United for £1 million. They made a poor start to the new season. They were tenth on the table in November and already being written off as title contenders.

Back then, there was no such thing as a transfer window. (FIFA's official transfer window became compulsory from 2002-03.) One drizzly afternoon in November 1992, Fergie found himself sitting with Chairman Martin Edwards pondering which player they might bid for, when Edwards' phone rang. It was Bill Fotherby, Chief Executive of Leeds United.

Fotherby wanted to buy United defender Denis Irwin. Edwards flatly rejected the request but, as the conversation generated into "friendly chit-chat", Fergie furiously scribbled "ask him about Eric Cantona" on a sheet of paper and thrust it under the Chairman's nose.

Cantona had shown glimpses of his brilliance in his short time at Leeds, but had a reputation for being quiet and difficult, and was not popular in the dressing room. There was unseemly gossip about his private life. One such rumour was that he was having an affair with the actress Leslie Ash, wife of Leeds teammate Lee Chapman. There are others which are unsafe to put into writing.

In 2003, Ash addressed the subject directly for the first time in a review of the television series *Footballers Wives*.

"A horrible rumour came out that I was having an affair with Eric Cantona after he left. They put it about that I was the reason Cantona left Leeds. Of course I didn't have an affair with him. The same thing happened to two other players' wives," Ash wrote.

There were also suggestions of a falling-out with between Cantona and manager Howard Wilkinson — the Frenchman would later say he couldn't "decode" what the Leeds boss was telling him.

Within half an hour, Fotherby phoned Edwards back to say they'd be prepared to do business over Cantona. Just a couple of days later, a £1 million deal was done. He was bought for the same price as Dublin.

Whatever the reason for the swift transfer, the moment the flawed Frenchman ambled into 'The Cliff', Manchester United's old training ground, the club's fortunes began to turn. If ever a player was born to play at the Theatre of Dreams, it was Cantona.

> His presence illuminated Old Trafford. Tall and straight-backed with the trademark upturned collar, he conveyed a regal authority and the place was in a frenzy every time he touched the ball.
>
> **– SIR ALEX FERGUSON**

By the time the 1992-93 season was over, United had beaten Aston Villa by a comfortable ten points and had romped to their first title in 26 years. They were dancing in the streets around Old Trafford.

After seven seasons at the helm, the temperamental — often terrifying — Scotsman had delivered the most sought-after prize in the English game. Along the way, he'd changed practically everything about Manchester United. Just as Ferguson had promised at the start of the season, the trophy which had for so long been owned by Liverpool or Arsenal was back where it belonged.

The signing of Cantona had been the decisive moment of that season — and one of the most decisive in the club's history. But there were other factors, factors which had United fans salivating at the prospect of sustained domination. Ryan Giggs was named the FA's Young Player of the Year and kids like David Beckham, Paul Scholes, Nicky Butt and the Neville brothers, Gary and Phil, were setting the world on fire in the Academy team.

The future looked as rosy as the manager's cheeks.

But, behind the scenes, Fergie was unhappy.

English Premier League 1992–93 Table								
Pos	Team	Pld	W	D	L	GF	GA	GD	Pts
1	Manchester United	42	24	12	6	67	31	+36	**84**
2	Aston Villa	42	21	11	10	57	40	+17	**74**
3	Norwich City	42	21	9	12	61	65	-4	**72**
4	Blackburn Rovers	42	20	11	11	68	46	+22	**71**

FORE!
WHERE WAS FERGIE WHEN THE DROUGHT-BREAKING 1992–93 TITLE WAS WON?

It might be an odd thing to say about a Scotsman (after all, they invented golf) but Sir Alex Ferguson is the last bloke you'd expect to be a golfer.

Just thinking about it, you can almost hear the shouts and see the clubs flying.

When Aston Villa hosted relegation-threatened Oldham Athletic on May 2, 1993, defeat for Villa would have handed the title to Manchester United for the first time since 1966-67. If Villa had won, United would have to beat Blackburn Rovers the following day to secure the trophy.

Fergie couldn't bring himself to watch the Villa-Oldham game, not even on TV. So, he did the next-most frustrating thing a football manager could do — he played golf.

Despite being on the precipice of history, Fergie took his oldest son Mark to Mottram Hall Golf Club near his Cheshire home, where Mark gave the old man a shot-a-hole handicap and wagered £5-a-hole on the result.

Fergie distinctly recalls taking in the spectacular view of the Cheshire countryside from the fourteenth fairway that fateful afternoon.

"I was gazing across the hills, waiting for four Japanese players ahead of us to take their shots when Mark said 'I think Villa have won. Someone would have told us if they'd lost.' I thought he was right."

By the time they were strolling up the seventeenth, Fergie's mind was a million miles from Villa Park.

"All I needed to do was halve the seventeenth and my money was safe. So, when I pitched up to within twenty feet of the hole, I was in a family mood and teasing Mark relentlessly," he recalls. Spoken like a true Scotsman.

"Suddenly I heard a car screeching to a halt and footsteps coming up the gravel path by the green and a chap appeared with a huge smile on his face."

> "'Mr Ferguson?' he called, and when I turned to him he shouted 'Manchester United have won the League.' (Oldham beat Villa 1—0.) Mark and I hugged each other. God, what a feeling."

Fergie couldn't bring himself to watch the Villa-Oldham game, not even on TV. So, he did the next-most frustrating thing a football manager could do –

↘**HE PLAYED GOLF.**

Despite having finally won the elusive championship he'd been dreaming of, Alex Ferguson was fighting a losing battle in his bid to become the best-paid manager in the division.

His friend and countryman, Arsenal manager George Graham, had leaked details of his own contract to Fergie, which revealed the United boss was being paid less than half of what Graham was taking home. Incidentally, Ferguson was earning less than a third of what United were paying Cantona.

Fergie had already admitted to taking a pay cut to move from Aberdeen to Manchester United in 1986. Now, almost seven years on, the club refused to budge on his demand for parity with the Arsenal boss. He signed an improved deal, but one which kept him way below what George Graham was making at Highbury.

For Fergie, the most sought-after rewards were always trophies. And in the 1993-94 season, he added a couple more to his burgeoning collection.

His first victory didn't bring any silverware, just a lot of satisfaction. It was over his old foes Kenny Dalglish and Jack Walker at Blackburn. Still smarting from missing out on Alan Shearer a year earlier, Ferguson wasn't going to lose the battle for the signature of a 21-year-old kid who'd caught his eye at Nottingham Forest — Roy Keane.

> There was an impressive resolve about the young Irishman and I knew he would not be deflected by

> the blandishments of Jack Walker.
> With Keane secured, I was optimistic
> that we were entering a period of
> dominance in English football.
>
> **– SIR ALEX FERGUSON**

United began the 1993-94 season with victory over Arsenal on penalties to claim the Charity Shield. But for a harsh red card to Andrei Kanchelskis in the League Cup final they might have had a second trophy before the end of March, losing to Aston Villa after the Russian was sent for an early bath for hand ball.

But, significantly, the title stayed at Old Trafford. Back-to-back Premier League crowns were sewn up on May 1 with victory over Ipswich at Portman Road, which gave Fergie plenty of time to prepare for an FA Cup final meeting with Chelsea. It turned out to be a leisurely stroll around Wembley. Three goals in nine minutes in the second half, plus a fourth in injury time, completed a phenomenal season. Manchester United had won the elusive 'double' for the first time.

The following season, 1994-95, Walker's millions finally earned Blackburn the title. Charity Shield aside (Fergie doesn't count them), United didn't pick up a trophy that season. Despite Blackburn slipping up at Anfield on the final day of the season, United's 1—1 draw at Upton Park left them a solitary point behind Rovers. A week later Everton pulled off a major upset and beat United 1—0 in the FA Cup final.

A frustrating season was typified by one cold, crazy afternoon at Selhurst Park in January 1995.

At half time of the match between United and Crystal Palace, Ferguson had warned his volatile superstar Cantona not to retaliate against the rough treatment he'd been receiving from Palace defender Richard Shaw. But, just four minutes into the second half, Cantona was sent off for lashing out at Shaw with his boot.

On the long walk back to the tunnel, Cantona responded to taunts from the home fans (it's alleged some threw tea bags at the Frenchman) by letting fly with his infamous kung fu kick, grazing Palace fan Matthew Simmons. Simmons later claimed he was walking to the toilet and was, simply, in the wrong place at the wrong time.

Cantona and Simmons briefly exchanged punches and both were punished. Simmons, who had a significant criminal record, was sentenced to a week's prison — he served one day. He was also fined £500 and banned from football grounds for a year.

Rightly or wrongly, Cantona's sentence was much more severe.

"Afterwards I ripped into Cantona with a fury I had vented only once before in our association," Fergie recalls.

United suspended the Frenchman for the final four months of the season and fined him £20,000. But, much to Fergie's fury, the Football Association added a further four months and £10,000 to the punishment. FIFA then insisted the ban should be world-wide, so he couldn't play abroad. To top it off, the French Football Federation stripped Cantona of the national captaincy.

The additional measures from the FA, FIFA and the FFF had Fergie fearing a mob mentality might hound his star out of football altogether.

"I don't think anyone in the history of football will get the sentence Eric got unless they had killed Bert Millichip's dog," Fergie famously said after the FA hearing into Cantona's behavior. (Millichip was FA chairman at the time.)

But if Fergie's canine quote became famous, Cantona's swipe at the media will surely never be beaten in terms of pure abstract artistry.

"When the seagulls follow the trawler, it's because they think sardines will be thrown into the sea. Thank you very much," he said.

In 2007 and long retired, Cantona remained unrepentant about that crazy afternoon against Palace.

> I have a lot of good moments, but the one I prefer is when I kicked the hooligan. I did not punch him strong enough. I should have punched him harder.
>
> **– ERIC CANTONA**

Respected football magazine *FourFourTwo* described the incident as something of a watershed in Manchester United's history: "It is almost a *Kennedy Assassination* moment for United fans. I can recall exactly what I was doing at the time; I was in the crowd, midway up the Arthur Wait Stand which was full of Reds. As the game went on, I couldn't take my eyes off him. He seemed to be seething inside, full of resentment."

Cantona was also charged with assault by police. At his hearing, he told the Croydon Crown Court that Simmons had insulted his mother in the crudest way possible. He was sentenced to two weeks prison, which was reduced to 120 hours community service on appeal.

He remained in football and played until 1997, retiring at the age of 30.

"I loved the game but I no longer had the passion to go to bed early, not to go out with my friends, not to drink, and not to do a lot of other things — the things I like in life."

At this point, it's easy to gloss over the trophies which began to arrive at Old Trafford on a conveyor belt. Winning had become a habit. In 1996-97, United became the first team to win the double twice. The following season they again won the title, despite ending a two-year unbeaten home run in the league and losing their first home game in Europe in 40 years.

With so much domestic success, the UEFA Champions League was becoming an obsession for Fergie. By the time the 1998-99 season began, his number one ambition was to make Manchester United the Kings of Europe, something the club had only ever achieved once, back in 1968 under Sir Matt Busby.

By the middle of the season, things weren't going well. On the eve of United's final Champions League group game against Bayern Munich, Fergie's loyal assistant Brian Kidd quit to become Blackburn manager. Ferguson didn't rush to replace him. Instead, he took control of training himself and was instantly reinvigorated.

United finished second to Bayern in the group stages, which meant they'd play a group winner in the quarter finals. Fergie relished the prospect. They were pitted against Inter Milan. After a comfortable 2—0 victory at Old Trafford, Paul Scholes earned the Red Devils a 1—1 draw at the San Siro. Another Italian nemesis awaited them in the semis: Juventus.

In the first half of the first leg at Old Trafford, United were played off the park by the team from Turin and were fortunate to be just one goal down. A late Ryan Giggs goal earned them a fluky draw. The return leg against Marcello Lippi's men was a classic.

After 11 minutes, United were two goals down and seemingly out of the tie. But Ferguson hadn't given up. To his horror, Roy Keane picked up a soft yellow card which meant he would miss the final if United could pull off a dramatic comeback.

Keane headed in United's first goal from a David Beckham corner. Dwight Yorke netted the equaliser just before half time as United took control of the game. Andy Cole scored the winner with six minutes left on the clock and United were into the final.

> **I didn't think I could have a higher opinion of a footballer than I already had of the Irishman (Keane) but he rose even further in my estimation at the Stadio Delle Alpi. The minute he was booked and out of the final, he seemed to redouble his efforts to get the team there.**
>
> **– SIR ALEX FERGUSON**

If the comeback in the semi was dramatic, United's revival in the final made the legend of Lazarus look like a brief, albeit biblical, snooze. Facing the might of Bayern Munich in the cauldron of Barcelona's Nou Camp, the Red Devils were again playing catch-up from the early stages. Mario Basler put the Germans in front with just six minutes gone, from a deflected free kick.

But they shut up shop and went defensive. Fergie sensed Bayern manager Ottmar Hitzfeld had made a mistake to attempt to defend for eighty-four minutes.

"After their goal went in, Bayern settled for a negative

policy of containment. Even when we over-committed ourselves in the search for an equaliser and left openings for counter-attacks that permitted them to hit our woodwork twice, they could not find the self-belief to come out and attempt to outplay us," Ferguson said.

Nonetheless, with 90 minutes gone and United still trailing by a single goal, Fergie was preparing to be "a good loser".

But the drama was only just beginning. Who could ever forget the sight of United keeper Peter Schmeichel charging down the pitch to ruffle the Bayern defenders at a corner? As a deafening roar went up, commentator Clive Tyldesley famously asked "Can Manchester United score? They always score!" And that's exactly what they did.

A Beckham corner brushed off Schmeichel and fell to Yorke. It was cleared by a flailing Thorsten Fink who put it directly into the path of Giggs. The Welshman blasted a shot from distance, which substitute Teddy Sheringham flicked past Bayern keeper Oliver Kahn. Kahn was left sitting on his backside with his left hand forlornly raised for off-side. Offside? Bollocks! It was 1—1.

If pandemonium reigned at the Nou Camp after 91 minutes, what followed was pure, unadulterated insanity. Fergie's new assistant Steve McLaren urged caution. "Now let's get ourselves organised for extra time. Go back to four, four, two," he suggested to Ferguson.

Fergie wasn't having any of that. "I said, 'Steve, this game isn't finished'."

Within seconds United had another corner and, while Schmeichel stayed put this time, there was an air of inevitability about what followed. It was the ultimate lesson in why a team should never sit on a one goal lead and just the dose of football justice the Germans deserved.

Sheringham headed the corner towards goal. The other 'super sub', Ole Gunnar Solskjaer, only had to stick out his leg and United were in dreamland. Up the other end, Schmeichel was doing cartwheels. Manchester United 2, Bayern Munich 1.

Back to Mr Tyldesley for the final word on an epic final:

> ## Manchester United have reached the promised land!
> ### – CLIVE TYLDESLEY

That same season, United held off Arsenal to win the League and beat Newcastle 2—0 in the FA Cup final. They had achieved the so-called impossible, the treble. Ferguson was on top of the world and in a league of his own.

Ever since the fateful season of 1998-99, the Premier League has almost become a battle to see if anyone can beat Manchester United. When others, namely Arsenal and Chelsea, have inevitably popped up with glimpses of glory, it has invariably been at United's expense. But Fergie has always bounced back.

Just as newly-rich Chelsea looked like it was issuing a lasting challenge to United's dominance with back-to-back titles in 2004-05 and 2005-06, Ferguson (who had become Sir Alex Ferguson by then) rose again, winning three titles in a row in 2006-07, 2007-08 and 2008-09.

The following season, United failed to win a record fourth-straight Premier League title by the narrowest of margins, Chelsea triumphing by a single point after an absorbing two-horse race to the finish line. It went some way to erasing the Londoners' agony of losing the Champions League final to Ferguson's men two years earlier.

In May 2008, on a chilly night in Moscow, United had broken Chelsea hearts to become Kings of Europe for a third time.

The circumstances were every bit as dramatic as they were in Barcelona nine years previously, although this time it was a slip from Chelsea captain John Terry in a penalty shoot-out which would deliver United another unlikely victory.

Yet Europe has remained a source of frustration for Sir Alex. In 2009, after humbling Arsenal in the semi-finals, United were brushed aside by Pep Guardiola's Barcelona in the final, losing 2—0 in Rome.

Two years later, against the same opponent at Wembley in London, it was the same story. Barcelona embarrassed United in a commanding 3—1 victory, choking the life out of the English club. Barca enjoyed a staggering 68 percent of time in possession and 22 shots on goal to United's 4.

It was a sad end to another title-winning season in 2010-11. With three games left to play, Chelsea had gone to Old Trafford with a chance of leapfrogging United into top spot in the table. But exciting young Mexican striker Javier "Chicharito" Hernandez struck in the very first minute and the Red Devils triumphed 2—1, to all-but secure the title.

The battles with Chelsea and the rise of other nouveau rich teams, like United's nearest neighbors Manchester City, will surely keep Sir Alex on his toes for as long as he wants, or needs, to keep going. But after a quarter of a century and having taken United to the summit of every conceivable footballing mountain, Fergie is simply adding greatness to greatness.

He may be a grumpy old bugger whose ranting about rival managers and referees has become almost comedic, but his place in the record books is safe.

It's now just a question of where to put the statue.

FERGIE'S MANAGERIAL TROPHY CABINET

Aberdeeen

1979-80	Scottish Premier Division
1981-82	Scottish Cup
1982-83	Scottish Cup
	UEFA Cup Winners Cup
1983-84	Scottish Premier Division
	Scottish Cup
	UEFA Super Cup
1984-85	Scottish Premier Division
1985-86	Scottish League Cup
	Scottish Cup

Manchester United

1989-90	FA Cup
1990-91	Charity Shield (shared with Liverpool)
	UEFA Cup Winners Cup
1991-92	UEFA Super Cup
	League Cup

1992-93	English Premier League
1993-94	Charity Shield
	English Premier League
	FA Cup
1994-95	Charity Shield
1995-96	English Premier League
	FA Cup
1996-97	Charity Shield
	English Premier League
1997-98	Charity Shield
1998-99	English Premier League
	FA Cup
	UEFA Champions League
1999-2000	English Premier League
	Intercontinental Cup
2000-01	English Premier League
2002-03	English Premier League
2003-04	Community Shield
	FA Cup
2005-06	League Cup
2006-07	English Premier League
2007-08	Community Shield
	English Premier League
	UEFA Champions League
2008-09	Community Shield
	FIFA Club World Cup
	League Cup
	English Premier League
2009-10	League Cup
2010-11	Community Shield
	English Premier League

How to be Ferocious like Fergie:

↘ Forgiveness is for Nancy Boys. If someone snubs you, don't get angry — get even. And never let them forget their mistake. In the fourteen years between the day Alan Shearer told Fergie where he could stick his offer to play at Manchester United and when the Geordie striker hung up his boots, United won 15 major trophies. Shearer won one.

↘ Timing is everything. Fergie would never have let a player like Eric Cantona leave his club for next to nothing just as he was entering his prime. With rumors of a personal rift with the manager and gossip about affairs with other players' wives, Leeds were vulnerable if a club came knocking for the Frenchman. Fergie swooped, and got him for a song. At least when he allowed Cristiano Ronaldo to leave Old Trafford at his peak some years later, he recouped 80 times what he'd paid for Cantona.

↘ Consider good fortune a God-given right. When John Terry slipped while taking a penalty, effectively handing United the 2008 Champions League title, Fergie didn't wax lyrical about how the artificial pitch and driving Moscow rain had come to his rescue. He simply declared that United had achieved their much-deserved destiny.

Timing is
↘ **EVERYTHING.**

WHEELER DEALER

What would you do with half a billion pounds? You could:

- Buy a Gulf Stream jet for you and each of your 11 closest friends.
- Slap a da Vinci on the sitting room wall and have enough left over for a van Gogh to put beside it.
- Build a bigger yacht than Roman Abramovich's *Eclipse* and, with the change, buy a twin engine chopper for the helipad and some toys for the hold.
- Spend 50,000 nights with the high-class hooker who claimed to have shagged a certain former Manchester United superstar in 2007.
- Check into the most expensive hotel penthouse on the French Riviera… and check out 76 years later.
- Extend your garage to squeeze in 3,000 Porsche 911s
- Pay off the national debt of Suriname.

Since his arrival at Old Trafford in 1986 Sir Alex Ferguson has spent more than £500 million on players.

But there hasn't always been a pile of blank cheques in his bottom drawer. When he started out in management all those years ago, he had to unearth players the hard way.

At East Stirlingshire his first trick was to send a bus to collect eager youngsters from around the neighbouring villages and towns, regardless of whether they lived in a rival club's territory. It was cheeky… and it worked.

He and his scouts used to travel the length and breadth of Scotland and England looking for hidden gems.

By the time he got to Old Trafford he'd built a network of scouts which covered all of Europe and beyond. In between Premier League matches, while his assistant coaches put the United players through their paces on the training track, Fergie would pop up to Oslo or across to Belgrade to check on the latest teen prodigy and schmooze the kid's parents.

He'd sit through endless hours of videos of players who'd been spotted by his scouts or were being touted by their manager.

But those were the good old days. Now, he picks up the phone and calls the Manchester United Accounts Department and demands a pile of cash.

Naturally, he still has to see a player and form an opinion, but the world is awake to the money on offer from Premier League clubs. Any kid worth a pinch of salt is on a scout's compilation reel somewhere. Or, more likely, there's an email from an agent sitting in Sir Alex's inbox. Although Fergie hates agents (presumably with the exception of his own son), they're now an integral part of the recruiting system.

Having said all that, in 2010 Sir Alex did something he'd never ever done before: he bought a player sight unseen. He paid £7.4 million for 20-year-old Portuguese attacking midfielder Bebe… without even watching a clip of the kid.

"On this occasion I didn't watch him. It is the first time I have done it," he confessed at the press conference to unveil the dreadlocked youngster.

"Normally I see plenty of video footage but our scouting department is very good and sometimes you have to go on instinct. Our scout in Portugal was adamant we must do something quickly."

His next step was to demand Bebe cut his hair.

But, after just one season, the gamble appeared to have failed, with the youngster written off by pundits as yet another expensive dud and shipped off to Turkish club Besiktas on loan.

Having turned Manchester United into the most successful club in the world, it isn't difficult for Sir Alex to convince a player to join him at Old Trafford. But he can expect even a youngster, through his manager or agent, to hit him up for a hundred thousand quid a week in wages. Furthermore, his original club will expect a six or seven figure transfer fee.

Publicly, Fergie hates the whole dirty business. He despises waste — he's a Scotsman, after all.

He was highly critical of Chelsea's spending in 2003-04 when Roman Abramovich arrived at Stamford Bridge and splashed out almost £100 million in a single summer. Never mind that Fergie spent £43.9 million during the same period, as well as £12.85 million on Louis Saha six months earlier during the January transfer window.

Seven years later, he condemned the way Manchester City splashed even more cash, more quickly after the Abu Dhabi prince, Sheikh Mansour, rolled into town in August 2008.

> Over the last two or three years we have seen very wealthy owners become part of football clubs and therefore go on this almost kamikaze effort to spend their money.
>
> – SIR ALEX FERGUSON

Could it be the man who could once outbid any club (with, perhaps, the exception of Real Madrid) is a tad jealous of the new rich kids on the Premier League block?

"It could be dangerous," he says. "But if they have that kind of money, they are certainly using it — I don't see it abating."

"We develop young players well and they have a loyalty towards you as they appreciate the education you give them as coaches."

True. As we've seen, Fergie's Academy was largely responsible for his success at Aberdeen in the 1980s and United in the mid-1990s. But he probably wouldn't have a single trophy in his cabinet without some serious commercial activity in the transfer market.

The truth is, when it comes to spending, Fergie's not so bad himself. The only real difference between Manchester United's spending and that of Manchester City and Chelsea is that United have spent their money a little slower. OK, a lot slower. But they've still spent it. And Ferguson is hardly renowned for bargain hunting like, say, Harry Redknapp or Sam Allardyce.

Here's a staggering list of his spending since arriving at Old Trafford in November 1986. It doesn't include every player he's bought, which would take the total well beyond half a billion pounds.

Also, it also doesn't include some of the large additional fees payable when a player reaches certain games or goals milestones, or the wads of cash given to the agents who buzz around clubs like flies around horse shit.

Naturally, of course, it is offset by players he's sold but, even taking into account the absurd £80 million Real Madrid paid for Cristiano Ronaldo in 2009, Fergie has still spent infinitely more than he's recouped.

TO FEE OR NOT TO FEE? ... THAT IS THE QUESTION

1987
Viv Anderson (Arsenal) £250,000
Brian McClair (Celtic) £850,000
Steve Bruce (Norwich City) £825,000

1988
Jim Leighton (Aberdeen) £750,000
Lee Sharpe (Torquay) £185,000
Mark Hughes (Barcelona) £1,800,000

1989
Mike Phelan (Norwich City) £750,000
Neil Webb (Nottingham Forest) £1,500,000
Gary Pallister (Middlesbrough) £2,300,000
Paul Ince (West Ham) £1,000,000
Danny Wallace (Southampton) £1,200,000

1990
Denis Irwin (Oldham Athletic) £625,000
Andrei Kanchelskis (Shakhtar Donetsk) £1,420,000

1991
Paul Parker (QPR) £2,000,000
Peter Schmeichel (Brondby) £530,000

1992
Dion Dublin (Cambridge United) £1,000,000
Eric Cantona (Leeds United) £1,000,000

1993
Roy Keane (Nottingham Forest) £3,750,000

1994
David May (Blackburn) £1,250,000

1995
Andy Cole (Newcastle United) £7,000,000

1996
Ronny Johnsen (Besiktas) £1,500,000
Karel Poborsky (Slavia Prague) £3,500,000
Ole Gunnar Solskjaer (Molde FK) £1,500,000
Jordi Cryuff (Barcelona) £1,400,000

1997
Teddy Sheringham (Tottenham) £3,500,000
Erik Nevland (Viking FK) £1,500,000
Henning Berg (Blackburn) £5,000,000

1998
Jonathan Greening (York City) £1,150,000
Jaap Stam (PSV Eindhoven) £10,750,000
Jesper Blomqvist (Parma) £4,400,000
Dwight Yorke (Aston Villa) £12,600,000

1999
Quinton Fortune (Atletico Madrid) £1,500,000
Massimo Taibi (Venezia) £4,500,000
Mikael Silvestre (Inter Milan) £4,000,000

2000
Fabien Barthez (Monaco) £7,800,000

2001
Ruud van Nistelrooy (PSV Eindhoven) £19,000,000
Juan Sebastian Veron (Lazio) £28,100,000
Roy Carroll (Wigan Athletic) £2,500,000

2002
Diego Forlan (Independiente) £7,500,000
Rio Ferdinand (Leeds United) £29,100,000
Ricardo (Valladolid) £1,500,000

2003
David Bellion (Sunderland) £2,000,000
Eric Djemba-Djemba (Nantes) £3,500,000
Tim Howard (Metro Stars) £2,300,000
Kleberson (Atletico Paranaense) £6,500,000
Cristiano Ronaldo (Sporting Lisbon) £12,200,000

2004
Louis Saha (Fulham) £12,850,000
Alan Smith (Leeds United) £7,050,000
Gabriel Heinze (Paris Saint-Germain) £6,900,000
Wayne Rooney (Everton) £30,000,000

2005
Edwin van der Sar (Fulham) £2,000,000
Park Ji-Sung (PSV Eindhoven) £4,000,000
Ben Foster (Stoke City) £1,000,000

2006
Nemanja Vidic (Spartak Moscow) £7,000,000
Patrice Evra (Monaco) £5,500,000
Michael Carrick (Tottenham) £18,600,000
Tomasz Kuszczak (West Bromwich Albion)
£2,125,000

2007
Owen Hargreaves (Bayern Munich) £17,000,000

Anderson (Porto) £17,000,000
Nani (Sporting Lisbon) £14,000,000
Carlos Tevez (loan — West Ham/private owner) £9,000,000

2008
Dimitar Berbatov (Tottenham) £30,750,000
Fabio & Rafael Da Silva (Fluminense) £5,200,000

2009
Zoran Tosic (Partizan Belgrade) £6,300,000
Antonio Valencia (Wigan Athletic) £16,000,000
Gabriel Obertan (Bordeaux) £3,000,000
Mame Biram Diouf (Molde FK) £4,000,000

2010
Marnick Vermijl (Standard Liege) £220,000
Chris Smalling (Fulham) £10,000,000
Javier Hernandez (Guadalajara) £7,000,000
Bebe (Vitoria Guimaraes) £7,400,000

2011
Anders Lindegaard (Aalesunds) £3,500,000
David De Gea (Atletico Madrid) £18,800,000
Phil Jones (Blackburn Rovers) £16,500,000
Ashley Young (Aston Villa) £16,000,000

Whether he likes it or not, Fergie has found himself in the middle of some of the most controversial — and questionable — transfer deals ever made.

No matter how strenuously he leaps to the defence of his son Jason's involvement in the strange arrangements to sell goalkeeping mega-flop Massimo Taibi and star defender Jaap Stam, there's no denying the deals were murky.

In the case of Taibi's move from Old Trafford to Reggina, records show that United paid £50,000 to the agency where Jason Ferguson worked, L'attitude. Yet Reggina's Chairman and Taibi's agent both told the BBC they had no dealings whatsoever with L'attitude.

When Stam moved suddenly to Lazio, Jason Ferguson's new agency, Elite, was paid a fee. Lazio were paid a fee and another UK-based agency received a fee. This is not to say anybody did anything illegal, it just underlines the nature of a business in which money changes hands in many directions on the back of a single deal.

In the transfer which brought Stam to Old Trafford in the first place, Fergie was accused of contacting the young defender while he was contracted to PSV Eindhoven — a practice the tabloid press have since labelled "tapping up". In his biography, *Head to Head*, Stam confesses to meeting Fergie in an Amsterdam apartment before United had made an official approach to PSV.

"He strode into the room, full of confidence and smiling broadly," Stam recalls.

"'Jaap, I want you to play for Manchester United,' he said. 'I want you to command our back line and help us to win the Champions League'. I was afraid he might have left the room with the wrong impression of me. At that time my English wasn't good and I could hardly understand his thick Scottish accent."

To be fair to United, they ended up making a very generous offer to PSV. The £10,750,000 they paid for him in 1998 made Stam the most expensive Dutch player in history (until they bought Ruud van Nistelrooy for almost twice that figure three years later).

> I think this is just the way Mr. Ferguson does things. If he wants to play at James Bond and arrange secret meetings in Amsterdam, there is nothing we can do about it.
>
> **– PEDRO SALAZAR-HEWITT,
> PSV EINDHOVEN SPOKESMAN**
> (On the Jaap Stam deal)

Ferguson has certainly had more successes than failures in the transfer market. But he hasn't always received value for money and, like most clubs, rarely sells at a profit. But three or four solid seasons out of any player — particularly if there are trophies involved — can be considered a healthy return on any transfer fee.

FERGIE'S FLOPS

Massimo Taibi

David May   Larent Blanc   William Prunier   Quinton Fortune

Jordi Cruyff   Juan Sebastian Veron   Eric Djemba-Djemba   Kleberson

Diego Forlan   David Bellion

Eric Cantona   Wayne Rooney

Ryan Giggs   Paul Scholes   Roy Keane   David Beckham

Denis Irwin   Jaap Stam   Steve Bruce   Gary Neville

Peter Schmeichel

FERGIE'S FLASHES

FLOPS VS FLASHES

Here's a comparison between Fergie's worst purchases and his best — including those he signed as kids and brought through United's Academy. First, the bad news — the flops:

FERGIE'S FLOPS XI

GOALKEEPER
Massimo Taibi
Bought for: £4,400,000
Sold for: £2,500,000
Games: 4
The 'Blind Venetian' ended up costing United £1.1 million per game. The lowlight of his brief career in red was a spectacularly disastrous performance against Chelsea, in which he had to pick the ball out of his net five times. Remembered as United's "worst keeper ever".

DEFENDERS
David May
Bought for: £1,200,000
Sold for: Free
Games: 90
Earned the dubious 'honour' of being named among *The Times'* 50 worst footballers of the Premiership era. His greatest contribution to the Red Devils' cause was an over-the-top celebration of the 1999 Champions League — of which he played zero minutes. "Utter tripe" is how one United fan described his career on *redcafe.net*. Harsh but fair.

Laurent Blanc
Bought for: Free
Sold for: Retired
Games: 71
At the age of 35, six years after Sir Alex first tried to bring him to Old Trafford, the Frenchman arrived on a free transfer from Inter Milan but failed to live up to his £2 million pay packet. Brought in to replace superstar Jaap Stam, he drew blank after blank after blank. From September 15 to December 1, 2001, United lost five games out of ten... to Bolton, Liverpool, Arsenal, Newcastle and Chelsea, which neatly spelled B-L-A-N-C. An embarrassing end to a brilliant career.

William Prunier
Brought for: Trial
Sold for: Free (no contract offered)
Games: 2
William who? The Frenchman features regularly in United 'Worst XI' discussions in chat rooms. He's often dismissed as a failed loan signing who, at least, didn't cost the club anything. Actually, United paid out his contract with Bordeaux to bring him in on trial and reunite him with his old pal Eric Cantona. A match made in hell.

Quinton Fortune
Bought for: £1,500,000
Sold for: Free
Games: 88
Perhaps a slightly harsh call, this one. Fortune was a genuine battler who was out of his depth at United. He couldn't maintain the fitness to hold his place at left back. Gabriel Heinze's arrival signaled the death knell for his time at Old Trafford. His career hit a deep downhill slide when he left Manchester United.

MIDFIELDERS
Jordi Cruyff
Bought for: £1,300,000
Sold for: Free
Games: 26
Good breeding is an excellent guide for judging racehorses, not footballers. If Cruyff's surname was Smith he'd never have gotten within a hundred miles of Old Trafford. The fans were certainly suspicious, chanting "Do it today... do it today... test Jordi's DNA". Last seen in a Genetic Laboratory in Zurich.

Juan Sebastian Veron
Bought for: £28,100,000
Sold for: £15,000,000
Games: 75
Arguably the worst purchase of Fergie's career, if only for the insane price tag. Despite dominating the Serie A with Lazio, Veron was too slow (and too *lazy*?) for the British game. What a waste of money. The fact that United fleeced £15 million out of Chelsea to take him off their hands is nothing short of a miracle. There's a great joke about Veron at the end of Chapter 9!

Eric Djemba-Djemba
Bought for: £3,500,000
Sold for: £1,350,000
Games: 27
One of many players brought in, unsuccessfully, to replace the irreplaceable Roy Keane. Given DJ-DJ's massive salary, Fergie couldn't get rid of him quick enough, shipping him off to Aston Villa where he was even worse. At various times during his brief career at United he was criticised for his shooting, passing, tackling and dribbling. Otherwise, he was great.

Kleberson
Bought for: £6,500,000
Sold for: £2,500,000
Games: 24
Arrived at Old Trafford with an escalated price tag and inflated reputation, following big Phil Scolari's glowing endorsement of his performance at the 2002 World Cup. Played just 20 League games in two years at Old Trafford, neither of which were title-winning seasons. These days fellow Brazilian Anderson is mocked by the Old Trafford crowd with chants of "Anderson-son-son — better than Kleberson-son-son". Ouch.

FORWARDS
Diego Forlan
Bought for: £7,500,000
Sold for: £2,000,000
Games: 37
Precisely why he failed so miserably at Manchester United remains one of football's great mysteries. It took Forlan eight long months to score his first goal in a red shirt — by which time he'd been lumbered with the nickname 'Diego Forlorn'. One clever pundit quipped after 27 goalless games in a row: "he couldn't hit a cow's rump with a banjo". It's little consolation to United fans that the Uruguayan became a superstar in Spain and was one of the stars of the 2010 World Cup.

David Bellion
Bought for: £2,000,000
Sold for: Free
Games: 15
Arrived from Sunderland in 2003 amid an ocean of controversy, with Sir Alex accused of tapping him

up. The Wearsiders should have been grateful. What a waste of time, energy and money. In 2007, the *Daily Mail* concluded: "Jesus. Bellion may not have been the worst player to wear a United shirt but he can't have been far off. Awful finishing and an attitude that stank."

FERGIE'S FLASHES XI

GOALKEEPER
Peter Schmeichel
Bought for: £530,000
Sold for: Free
Games: 400
At various times of his glittering career, the Great Dane was voted United's "Greatest Goalkeeper Ever" and the "Best Goalkeeper in the World". A giant between the posts for club and country, he won three Danish titles, collected five Premier League winners' medals, was an integral member of the 1999 treble winning team and helped Denmark win Euro '92. Taibi couldn't do up his bootlaces.

DEFENDERS
Gary Neville
Bought for: Free (trainee)
Sold for: Retired
Games: 602
You probably wouldn't buy a used car from him or take him out for a pint, but Neville's undying devotion to the United cause was beyond question. He won more silverware in two decades at Old Trafford than most clubs win in a century and retired in 2011 as United's (and England's) most capped right-back.

Steve Bruce
Bought for: £825,000
Sold for: Free
Games: 414
One of the all-time great Manchester United defenders. His partnership with Gary Pallister was the backbone of Ferguson's transformation of the club in the late 1980s and early 1990s. Won seven trophies at United and went on to become an established manager in his own right.

Jaap Stam
Bought for: £10,750,000
Sold for: £16,500,000
Games: 125
During his time at Old Trafford he was arguably the best defender in the world. His premature departure from the club after the release of his highly un-controversial biography *Head to Head* was possibly the biggest mistake Fergie ever made in the transfer market. Even Ferguson admitted he should never have allowed the big Dutchman to leave. Yes, Fergie admitted he was wrong — rare, indeed. Shows how highly he rated Stam.

Denis Irwin
Bought for: £625,000
Sold for: Free
Games: 513
Look up 'dependable' in the dictionary and you might just find a photo of the man who won seven League titles at left back for United. While he wasn't a flashy player by any stretch of the imagination, he was a dead-ball demon. Despite all the superstar strikers he played alongside, he was United's penalty taker for most of his career. A fan's dream.

MIDFIELDERS

David Beckham
Bought for: Free (trainee)
Sold for: £25,000,000
Games: 359
Although he may have been surpassed by Cristiano Ronaldo in terms of natural talent, Beckham gave the best years of his life to United. A football prodigy who became the most marketable sportsman in the world, he was a free-kick maestro. He single-handedly won many, many important games for United and England.

Roy Keane
Bought for: £3,750,000
Sold for: Free
Games: 458
The ultimate football warrior. He scared the crap out of rival midfielders. His endurance and toughness as captain inspired his teammates to even greater heights. He was involved in some of football's great bust-ups, too. Ireland manger Mick McCarthy sent him packing from the 2002 World Cup after he reportedly told the Gaffer, in front of the entire team: "Mick, you're a liar... you're a fucking wanker. I didn't rate you as a player, I don't rate you as a manager, and I don't rate you as a person. You're a fucking wanker and you can stick your World Cup up your arse." He watched the rest of the event on television.

Paul Scholes
Bought for: Free (trainee)
Sold for: Retired
Games: 554*
(Before you start writing angry emails, remember...

Bryan Robson was already at Old Trafford when Fergie arrived.)
Another graduate of the 1992 Youth FA Cup victory, Scholes was nominated by none other than Zinedine Zidane as one of his all-time favorite players. "Paul Scholes is the complete midfielder. He is undoubtedly the best midfielder of his generation," the great Frenchman said. It's a monstrous call... but who's arguing?

Ryan Giggs
Bought for: Free (trainee)
Games: 757*
Fergie famously described the day he first laid eyes on the left-footed Welshman: "He was 13 and just floated over the ground like a Cocker Spaniel chasing a piece of silver paper in the wind." You could get arrested for saying something like that these days. Giggs has been involved in more trophy victories than any other player in United's (or Fergie's) history. One of the world's greatest left wingers.

FORWARDS
Wayne Rooney
Bought for: £30,000,000
Games: 287*
The difference between coming through Everton's Academy and coming through Manchester United's Academy is, obviously, thirty million quid. When Cristiano Ronaldo left for Real Madrid in 2009, Rooney confirmed himself as United's most influential player, delivering an awesome season. Despite a temper to match that of his manager, Rooney is among the most powerful strikers ever to represent United.

Eric Cantona
Bought for: £1,000,000
Sold for: Retired
Games: 190
The King. The single most important player of the Ferguson era. Without him, Fergie's career might have ended 15 years ago. One of the most naturally gifted players in history — he now enjoys icon status at Old Trafford alongside Busby, Charlton, Best and Ferguson.

FERGIE'S FLOPS VS FERGIE'S FLASHES

GAMES:	459	5,659*
PAID:	£56,000,000	£47,480,000
RECOUPED:	£23,350,000	£41,500,000
LOST:	£32,650,000	£5,980,000

THE KING. The single most important player of the Ferguson era. Without him, Fergie's career might have ↘**ENDED 15 YEARS AGO.**

GAZZA-UMPED – THE ONES THAT GOT AWAY

> **Mr Ferguson, you go and enjoy your holiday. I am signing for Manchester United when you come back.**
>
> **– PAUL GASCOIGNE, JUNE 1988**

With those comforting words Alex Ferguson jetted off to Malta for a hard-earned summer holiday with his family.

As he soaked up the Mediterranean sun he was confident that when the 1988-89 season began, with Gascoigne in his ranks, he'd have a team that could finally end Manchester United's long wait for a First Division title.

The poolside pina coladas must never have tasted sweeter. That was, until his name was announced on the hotel public address system (this was before the time when everyone had global roaming... or a mobile phone). Someone needed him — urgently. It was United Chairman Martin Edwards calling from Manchester.

"Gascoigne has signed for Spurs," announced the voice on the end of the phone. Fergie was lost for words. He had the next-best thing to a contract: verbal assurance from the player himself. No-one changed their mind after giving Fergie their word. No-one until Gazza.

"Paul's feelings were swung when Tottenham bought a house for his parents," Ferguson recalls.

In retrospect, Fergie felt that not only could Gascoigne have been a bigger star at United than he was at Tottenham, he might have avoided the slippery slope into alcoholism, violence, depression and crime which destroyed his career and, on several occasions, almost cost the Tynesider his life.

"Could I have helped him? Well I think about what we would have taken away — we'd have taken London out of the road for him," Ferguson said in 2008.

"We had Bobby Charlton, a Geordie, Bryan Robson, a Geordie, Steve Bruce, a Geordie. We had a structure of players who could have helped him and I think it would have given him some discipline."

In 2009, Gascoigne revealed Fergie wasn't the only one regretting his change of heart back in the summer of '88.

"I got invited to the Academy and it is a magnificent place and you can see the way he treats his players. He treats them with respect but he also makes men out of boys," Gascoigne said.

"Maybe if I had stayed at Man. United I might have still been there. I don't know, you just look at these players and the squad of young kids the way he (Ferguson) just brought them on and there are so many."

"It took me six years to get back talking to Sir Alex. I called him from Lazio and asked him would he re-sign (me). He was with Eric Cantona and he said he would see what Cantona was going to do but I think everyone knows if you do something to Sir Alex Ferguson the way I did you don't get a second chance."

Everyone knows
if you do something to
Sir Alex Ferguson the way I did
YOU DON'T GET A ↙
SECOND CHANCE.

Gascoigne wasn't the only big name to slip through Sir Alex's fingers. Forget all the nonsense you read each summer about players being "linked with" Manchester United, the following are the top ten players Fergie himself admits trying to sign... and failing.

1. Paul Gasgoigne — See above.

2. Alan Shearer — See chapter 5.

3. Ronaldinho — With pockets bulging from the sale of David Beckham in 2003, Fergie dispatched chief executive Peter Kenyon to Lyon to bid for the hottest property in football, Ronaldinho, who was being sold by Paris St-Germain. According to an unauthorised biography on the Brazilian, the story goes that Kenyon outbid Barcelona and agreed a deal of €30 million with the French club. But Kenyon discovered he'd been played-off against Barca director Sandro Rosell, who'd dropped out of the bidding at €27 million. So, when he faxed the paperwork the next day he made the price €28 million instead of €30 million, infuriating PSG, who promptly rang Barca and did the deal for €27 million.

4. Fernando Torres — Just six months after Torres signed for Liverpool, Fergie revealed his frustration at missing out on the Spanish striker. "For years we tried to do a deal there but we never quite managed it because Atletico Madrid didn't want to sell. Then we just lost interest a bit because sometimes you get fed up with going back to the same venue all the time."

5. Pep Guardiola — Fergie tried to lure the man who would become his managerial nemesis away from Barcelona in 2001. The Spaniard's agent said "Pep's contract was ending in June 2001. Alex Ferguson's son, Jason, called me the previous October to say United were keen. Pep liked what he saw. Ferguson wanted a meeting with Pep (but) it was cancelled as United were angry things were taking too long."

6. Paolo Maldini — "I always wanted to get Paolo here but it was impossible," Ferguson told *The Sun* in January 2010. "I met his father at a game and told him how much I'd love to have his son at United. Cesare (Maldini) smiled at me and said 'my grandfather was Milan, my father was Milan, I played for Milan and now my son is Milan'. And that was it — story over."

7. John Barnes — Watford manager Graham Taylor offered Barnes to Ferguson for £900,000 in 1987. Fergie declined, as a show of faith to United's Danish winger Jesper Olsen. When Olsen flopped, he turned to Ralph Milne from Bristol City. Fergie now admits that Milne's name is "enshrined in the fan folklore of United as the symbol of bad buying". He was a disaster. Missing out on Barnes remains one of Fergie's great transfer regrets.

8. Nicholas Anelka — In November 2007 Fergie revealed: "I have tried to buy him several times. We always assess players with pace and ability to score and he comes into that category. He has done it throughout his career."

9. Peter Beardsley — Ferguson approached Newcastle United for the signature of Beardsley and got a 'frosty' response from manager Willie McFaul. "He said there was no way Beardsley would be sold to us even if we offered £3 million. The next week the little forward went to Liverpool for £1.9 million."

10. Arjen Robben — When Robben was playing for PSV Eindhoven he was contacted by Fergie, who followed up with a formal €7 million bid. PSV Chairman Harry van Raaij rejected the offer out of hand and accepted almost three times that from Chelsea a few weeks later.

CAN YOU SPARE SOME CHANGE PLEASE?

The name Rune Hauge still sends shivers down Sir Alex Ferguson's spine.

The bespectacled Norwegian might look like a mild-mannered refrigerator salesman — in fact, he's the most controversial agent in European football.

He was the man at the centre of the "bungs" scandal which cost former Arsenal manager George Graham his job at Highbury. The Scandinavian was banned for life by FIFA, a sentence which was later reduced to a two-year suspension of his license.

Years later, Hauge was named in court documents following the messy transfer of Jon Obi Mikel from Lyn Oslo to Chelsea, despite the Nigerian signing a contract to join Manchester United.

These days — somehow — Hauge's still making a killing (well, a living) from football, as a middleman in the sale of Premier League rights around Scandinavia.

Fergie endured his own dealings with Hauge, one of which resulted in him being handed a gift-wrapped box containing £40,000 cash. Hauge had introduced him to the agents of Andrei Kanchelskis, who negotiated the transfer of the Russian winger from Shakhtar Donetsk to Manchester United in 1991. When the impressive Kanchelskis signed an extension to his contract in 1994 and scored a brilliant goal early in the 1994-95 campaign, the Russian's agent insisted on giving Fergie the gift, which he didn't open until he got home.

"At first I didn't know what to do, but Cathy said I should return the money to (the agent, Grigory) Essaoulenko immediately and that seemed sensible. Then alarming thoughts began to jump into my head. What if my meeting with Grigory had been filmed? I needed a witness to this madness."

The cash was eventually locked in a safe at Manchester United, where it remained for a year until it could be given back to the bemused — and somewhat confused — Russian.

Fergie has often bemoaned the role of agents in modern football, but he probably doesn't concur with former Crystal Palace owner Simon Jordan who took a swipe at Fergie and agents in the same breath.

"Agents are nasty scum. They're evil and divisive and pointless," Jordan told the *News of the World*.

"They only survive because the rest of the sport is so corrupt and because leading football club people employ their sons in the job."

How to be Ferocious like Fergie:

⬎ If you stayed up all night watching reruns of *River City* and can't be shagged watching hours of lower-league Portuguese football on DVD, just buy the young midfielder your scout has been hounding you about. What's £7 million between friends? The kid must be OK. It sure beats the hell out of another mid-week winter trip to Los Drossos, Portugal — even in a private jet.

⬎ Spend half a billion quid of someone else's money then cry blue murder when someone else dares to start outbidding you in the transfer market. If you miss out on a player to one of your rich rivals, call a press conference and mock the transfer fee they paid as 'grossly excessive', then mumble a lot about Ryan Giggs, Paul Scholes, David Beckham and the Nevilles. If someone tries to blame you for the Veron, Kleberson or Forlan disasters, feign early-onset Alzheimer's.

⬎ Beware of agents bearing gifts. There is always, always a catch.

BEWARE of agents bearing gifts. There is always,
⬎**ALWAYS A CATCH.**

"I WILL LOVE IT IF WE BEAT THEM"
– THE RIVALRIES

For a man who loves nothing more than taking an adversary into his office after a game to chew the fat and slurp fine wine, Sir Alex Ferguson has managed to upset a multitude of managers over the years.

To Manchester United fans, Fergie's bloody-minded, win-at-all-costs mentality has delivered almost endless joy. But it has come at a price: he is not popular among his peers and even less so among rival fans. He is hated by sections of the media and despised by referees.

He will never be remembered with the same warmth as someone like Sir Bobby Robson, Bob Paisley or Sir Mat Busby. Even Jose Mourinho, that very essence of arrogance, is admired for his colourful style and sharp wit.

Fergie's snarling demeanour and refusal to accept he's ever been tactically out-manoeuvred — not to mention his utter contempt for anyone who dares challenge him — has ensured his legacy will always be clouded.

Undoubtedly, trophies and success have brought him respect, albeit begrudging, from rivals over the years. And, certainly, old age has mellowed him.

But, even now, when he explodes on the touchline or makes yet another ridiculous claim of bias in a post-match media conference, it's easy to dislike him — plenty of his contemporaries seem to. Throughout his long career, Sir Alex has ruffled the feathers of even the most mild-mannered managers and players.

"He is a brilliant psychologist. He knows what to say at the right moment. He knows the art of rattling his opponent," says Fergie's biographer, Michael Crick.

Scottish football commentator Archie Macpherson says

'Doctor' Ferguson was "playing shrink" long before he arrived at Old Trafford.

"Putting in a word here and there in the press about your opponent, aggravating them... you could go through a whole host of managers he did that with. And why? Because he wants to win."

Here are some of the egos he's dented, the noses he's put out of joint, the tall poppies he's chopped down and the skins he's effortlessly crawled under.

Arsene Wenger

Mostly, Fergie's mind games are not personal. But, in the case of Arsene Wenger, he was happy to make an exception. In the early 2000s their bickering was nothing short of venomous.

> **Ferguson should calm down. Maybe it would have been better if he had put us against a wall and shot us.**
> – ARSENE WENGER, OCTOBER 2004

Without doubt, Ferguson and Wenger are the greatest rivals in the short history of the Premier League. They might not hate each other any more, but they undeniably used to. There was a time when one couldn't open his mouth without irritating the other.

When the Frenchman sauntered into Highbury in 1996, Ferguson poked fun at his hawkish reputation as a football 'professor', lambasting his linguistic skills as nothing terribly special. He continued to slate Wenger at every opportunity during their first season of battle. "He's a novice — he should keep his opinions to Japanese football," Fergie declared, taking a shot at Wenger's previous managerial appointment with Nagoya Grampus in Japan.

The following season, Wenger complained bitterly when United were given an extended break following a Champions League fixture. "It's wrong the league program is extended so Man. United can rest up and win everything," he fumed.

But those little exchanges were merely an hors d'oeuvre when compared with what the pair dished up at the peak of their rivalry between 2003 and 2005.

By that stage, Wenger had won two league titles and was about to add a third. The Gunners boss delighted in reminding Ferguson that, unlike United, his team always played beautiful football... even when they weren't winning.

It clearly hit a raw nerve. "They are scrappers who rely on belligerence. We are the better team," Fergie said. Wenger responded with a gem: "Everyone thinks they have the prettiest wife at home."

In September 2003, there were ugly scenes after a match between United and Arsenal at Old Trafford. Fergie's star striker Ruud van Nistelrooy had missed a late penalty. At the final whistle, the Arsenal players let the Dutchman know all about it, jostling him roughly as he left the pitch.

Ferguson was furious: "They got away with murder. What the Arsenal players did was the worst I have witnessed in sport."

"Arsenal are the worst losers of all time," he said the following season.

It all spilled over in October 2004, the day Arsenal's record unbeaten run of 49 league games came to an end. It will forever be remembered as 'Pizzagate'.

The post-script to the Ferguson-Wenger soap opera is that now they actually get along reasonably well. The success of a mutual enemy, Chelsea, and the departure of some of the more combative players from both teams has seen a rare outbreak of peace between Old Trafford and the Emirates Stadium.

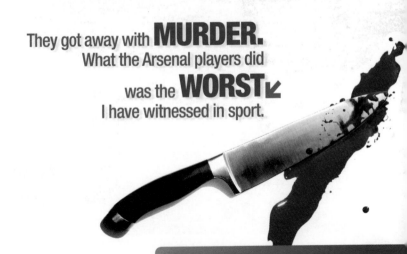

They got away with **MURDER.**
What the Arsenal players did
was the **WORST**
I have witnessed in sport.

'PELTED WITH PEPPERONI' – WHO THREW THE PIZZA THAT ENDED UP ON FERGIE'S FACE?

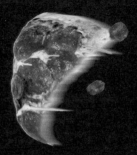

"This slice of pizza came flying over my head and hit Fergie straight in the mush. The slap echoed down the tunnel and everything stopped – the fighting, the yelling, everything. All eyes turned and all mouths gawped to see this pizza slip off that famous puce face and roll down his nice black suit."

– ASHLEY COLE
(From his 2006 autobiography, *My Defence*)

> **Nobody threw the pizza. It flew alone.**
> — ARSENE WENGER, 2004

> **Jens Lehmann and Thierry Henry were among the rumoured culprits, but over time the finger of blame has come to be pointed at the cherubic Francesc Fabregas.**
> — OLIVER KAY, *THE TIMES*, 2005

It all began, oddly enough, with a game of football.

The Gunners were beaten 2—0 in another physical encounter at Old Trafford. Wenger was devastated at being denied what would have been a magical milestone: fifty league games without a loss. But he was more up in arms about the nature of the defeat.

United had gone ahead in the first half through a van Nistelrooy penalty after Wayne Rooney was felled in the box. Arsenal keeper Jens Lehmann declared "we lost to a Rooney dive". It's a view which has been echoed by Gunners' players and fans ever since. On the touchline, Wenger had conniptions. Rooney doubled United's lead with a goal in the second half to seal the points.

"In all my sporting life, I have never received so many kicks as I did in Manchester. It was the hardest match I have played," complained Arsenal's Jose Antonio Reyes afterwards. Ferguson insisted Reyes was only fouled four times, while his own young star, Cristiano Ronaldo, was fouled eight times.

As the teams marched up the tunnel after the final whistle, Wenger waited for van Nistelrooy and shouted at him. He accused him of cheating — an accusation he repeated on live television (which earned him a rap over the knuckles from the FA). Ferguson emerged from the United dressing room to defend his Dutch striker and it was on for young and old... literally.

Wenger is said to have given the United boss a frightful mouthful in a combination of English and French. But, just when it looked like the managers might start swinging punches, it came to an abrupt end. As if in slow motion, a slice of pizza sailed out of the Arsenal dressing room and plopped onto Fergie's red face, then slid down his front.

Embarrassed, and wearing an unsightly mozzarella mask, Fergie slunk back into the United dressing room.

"Ferguson's out of order. He has lost all sense of reality. He is going out looking for a confrontation, then asking the person he is confronting to apologise. He's pushed the cork in a bit far this time," Wenger said.

Fergie responded by giving a public account of the 'Pizzagate' affair. He claimed Wenger had exploded in a fit of rage after he'd calmly told the Frenchman to "behave himself".

> **He ran** at me with his hands raised saying 'What do you want to do about it?' To not apologise for the behaviour of the players to another manager is unthinkable. It's a disgrace, but I don't expect Wenger to ever apologise... he's that type of person.
>
> **– SIR ALEX FERGUSON**

In the days after the controversy, newspapers competed to get the inside story of 'The Battle of the Buffet'. Ashley Cole was the main suspect. Jens Lehmann and Thierry Henry were next in the firing line. But it wasn't until Cole released his autobiography, *My Defence*, two years later, that the world finally reached a consensus on a culprit.

"All I can say is that the culprit wasn't English or French, so that should narrow it down," Cole wrote, clearly pointing the finger of blame at Cesc Fabregas, who did not deny his involvement.

So, the schoolboy prank of the decade was indeed carried out by a schoolboy. It was a teenage Spaniard who delivered the goods in Fergie's most famous food fight.

Kenny Dalglish

Although Fergie delighted in his verbal sparring with Brian Clough and the man he replaced at Old Trafford, Ron Atkinson, the main focus of his anger during his first decade at Old Trafford was Kenny Dalglish.

When you manage United, it's your job to hate Liverpool... and Fergie took up the task with relish. Remember, Fergie stated his number one ambition at United was "knocking Liverpool off their fucking perch". When he arrived at Old Trafford, Dalglish was in charge at Anfield and, when 'King Kenny' later moved to Blackburn, the battles were equally barbaric.

> You might as well talk to my baby daughter (than Alex Ferguson). You'll get more sense out of her.
> — KENNY DALGLISH, to a reporter in 1988

The rivalry dates back to Fergie's time as assistant coach, then manager, of Scotland; most notably Dalglish's reaction to Fergie's decision to leave Alan Hansen out of the 1986 Mexico World Cup squad.

Dalglish and Hansen were close friends. Just as the Scottish squad was about to fly out, Dalglish withdrew from the team — some say in protest at the axing of Hansen, although Kenny insisted he needed knee surgery.

Fergie would later accuse Dalglish, the player, of failing on the biggest stage of all, saying his fellow Scotsman never "set the heather on fire" at the three previous World Cups.

Eventually, Fergie agreed to write the foreward to Dalglish's autobiography, *My Autobiography*. It was his famous "guide to death" in which he accused Kenny of having barely enough true friends to carry his coffin.

Ironically, Dalglish was back in charge at Anfield in 2011, just in time to see Sir Alex fulfil his great wish of knocking Liverpool off their perch. Manchester United's 19th league title broke Liverpool's long-standing record of 18.

Kevin Keegan

It was like watching a car wreck in slow motion.

When Kevin Keegan crumbled under the television lights at Elland Road, Leeds, on 29 April, 1996, it signalled the ultimate psychological victory of Sir Alex Ferguson's career as a manager.

Keegan's humiliation remains one of the all-time great football outbursts. It was voted "quote of the decade" in a poll on the FA's official website in 2003.

At the time, Keegan was in charge of Newcastle United. His team had somehow managed to throw away a 10-point lead at the top of the table in just three short months. Clearly, being mowed down by Manchester United had taken its toll on the normally-affable Keegan.

A week earlier Fergie had, somewhat casually, mentioned that he felt teams tried harder against United than they did against Newcastle. It was a typical, not-so-subtle hint to Newcastle's next opponents, Leeds United, to give their best against Keegan's men. Keegan blew his top.

Not surprisingly, the headline writers were ruthless: "Keegan in danger of cracking under the strain" shouted *The Independent*. "Keegan Crumbles" wrote *The Sun*.

Fergie would later express his regret at Keegan's embarrassment, but cheekily admitted his little jibe achieved a bullseye. "I think I helped stiffen their (Leeds') resolve by focusing so much attention on them," he said.

Although Newcastle beat Leeds 1—0 that fateful night, the Geordies were clearly rattled. United won the title and, by halfway through the following season, Keegan was out of a job.

> You can tell him now, if you're watching it, we're still fighting for this title and he's got to go to Middlesbrough and get something. And, I'll tell you honestly, I will love it if we beat them. Love it.
>
> – KEVIN KEEGAN, APRIL 29, 1996

Rafael Benitez

> Only Mr. Ferguson can talk about the fixtures, can talk about referees, can talk about all these things, and nothing happens. I think they were thinking that we would not be at the top of the table in January and we are top of the table. So, clearly, they are nervous.
>
> **— RAFAEL BENITEZ, JANUARY 2009**

You'd think after Keegan's public humiliation that rival managers might be a little wary of walking into one of Fergie's mental minefields. But that's exactly what Liverpool manager Rafael Benitez did in early 2009.

Responding to Ferguson's suggestion that the Reds might choke as the battle for the 2008-09 title went down to the wire, Benitez pulled some notes out of his back pocket and delivered his infamous 'Rafa rant' at a press conference. Among his many allegations, he suggested Manchester United received favourable treatment by officials... on and off the pitch.

Just as Keegan had done thirteen years earlier, the outburst was interpreted as a rival manager falling victim to Fergie's psychological warfare.

History shows that Liverpool were, indeed, gobbled up by United at the end of the season. Fergie's men won the title by four points. A season later, Benitez left Anfield for Inter Milan where he lasted just six months before being fired again.

Gordon Strachan

> **I decided this man could not be trusted an inch. I would not want to expose my back to him in a hurry.**
>
> – SIR ALEX FERGUSON

Fergie and Strachan have been at each other's throats since 'wee Gordie' played under Sir Alex with Aberdeen, Scotland and Manchester United in the 1970s and '80s.

When Fergie discovered Strachan was plotting to leave Pittodrie behind his back in 1984, he launched a bitter attack: "Though I always felt there was a cunning streak in Strachan, I had never imagined that he could pull such a stroke on me."

In return, when Strachan became a manager himself, he hinted that Ferguson deliberately played a below-strength team in Manchester United's final fixture of the 2000-01 season against Derby to ensure Strachan's Coventry were relegated, which they were.

Sven-Goran Eriksson

When Fergie changed his mind (with the help of Lady Cathy) about retiring in 2002, many felt it was because he didn't want some of those being touted as his replacement to fill his shoes at Old Trafford — including Strachan and former England manager Eriksson.

> I think Sven would have been a nice easy choice for them. Nothing really happens. He doesn't change anything. He sails along. Nobody falls out with him. 'The first half we were good, second half we were not so good – I am very pleased with the result'.

– SIR ALEX FERGUSON

Jose Mourinho

Mourinho always claimed to have had Fergie's measure, tactically, but was careful not to be openly critical of the ferocious Scot. He would preface his own Fergie-like sermons with "I like Sir Alex, he is my friend", before tearing strips off United.

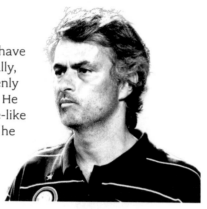

> **He was certainly full of it, calling me 'boss' and 'big man' when we had our post-match drink after the first leg. But it would help if his greetings were accompanied by a decent glass of wine. What he gave me was paint-stripper.**
>
> **– SIR ALEX FERGUSON**

TOP 10 FERGIE QUOTES

1. *"When an Italian tells me it's pasta on the plate I check under the sauce to make sure. They are the inventors of the smokescreen."*
   Fergie upsets the whole of Italy ahead of United's Champions League clash with Juventus, 1999.

2. *"You scumbag, you ratbag, you dirty bastard."*
   PSV Eindhoven's Paul Bosvelt feels Fergie's wrath after his horror tackle on Denis Irwin during a Champions League tie, 1997.

3. *"It's getting tickly now — squeaky-bum time, I call it."*
   Fergie adds a new phrase to the football lexicon, 2003.

4. *"You're a fuckin' bottler Incey! You cannae handle the stage, can you? You are a fuckin' bottler."*
   To Paul Ince at half-time of a disastrous 4—0 Champions League defeat at the Nou Camp, 1994.

5. *"If he was an inch taller he'd be the best centre half in Britain. His father is 6ft 2in. I'd check the milkman."*
   Ferguson questions the parentage of Gary Neville, 1996.

6. *"He could start a fight in an empty house."*
   Fergie describes Chelsea's pesky captain, Dennis Wise, 1997.

7. *"Ashley Cole made you look a cunt."*
   To David Beckham after an FA Cup loss to Arsenal, 2003. Beckham's response: *"And Wenger made you look like a cunt... again."*

8. *"I can understand why clubs come away from Anfield choking on their own vomit and biting their tongues knowing they have been done by the referee."*
   The love affair with Anfield begins, 1988.

9. *"We're suffering because of what happened against Arsenal... one of my players would have to be hit by an axe to get a penalty at the moment."*
   Fergie's not-so-subtle criticism of the referee after beating Arsenal, 2004.

10. *"Do you think I would enter into a contract with that mob? No chance. I would not sell them a virus."*
    Ferguson denies the deal to sell Cristiano Ronaldo had been done long before C-Ron moved to Real Madrid, 2009.

One of my players would have to be HIT BY AN AXE ↙ to get a PENALTY at the moment.

NO GREATER HATER – PIERS MORGAN

Piers Morgan is best known for being a talent-show judge with a soft touch.

He's the one who championed the cause of Susan Boyle, a shy lass from Scotland who dared to publicly dream her dream on *Britain's Got Talent* in 2009.

But there's nothing soft about Morgan's opinion of Boyle's fellow Scot, Sir Alex Ferguson.

The pair famously fell out when Morgan was editor of *The Mirror* and published extracts of Jaap Stam's biography, much to Fergie's fury.

In 1999, after Ferguson was stopped by police for driving on the hard shoulder of a motorway, he was let off without charge because he claimed to have been suffering acute diarrhea. Arsenal fan Morgan jokingly sent him a bottle of Imodium and a note saying: "We Gooners knew you were always full of crap, and now we've got the proof."

Fergie didn't see the humour. From then on, their relationship went downhill.

In 2008, the normally good-tempered Morgan gave Sir Alex a frightful spray in his *Daily Mail* column: "Let me start this column how I mean to continue: I hate Sir Alex Ferguson. I don't just mean I mildly dislike the man; I mean I completely and utterly detest him. And I say that with all the calm, dispassionate authority of an Arsenal season-ticket holder."

An *Independent* reporter recalls trying to broker a peace deal on Morgan's behalf, asking the Manchester United boss if there was anything he could do to mend the relationship.

"Yes," Ferguson reportedly told him. "You can fuck off and die."

How to be Ferocious like Fergie:

- Don't wear your most expensive suit for matches against Arsenal. If you do, put on a bib and crash helmet for the walk down the tunnel.

- Subtlety will get you nowhere. Understatement is for pansies. If you think an opposition player dived or had one of your players sent off, don't fanny about hinting that the boy "made the most of it". Just brand him a cheat and be done with it.

- Always hold a grudge. Grudges are good. If you're going to manage until you're a hundred and five years old, there will always be an opportunity for revenge.

- Toss a verbal hand grenade at a rival manager just when he's about to crumble. Uncork a bottle of decent Chateau Figeac, sit back on the sofa and watch the carnage unfold on TV. You'll sleep like a baby.

- Simply winning is not enough. Grind your opponent into the ground. Shame him, embarrass him and ridicule him. True victory is when it's you holding the cup and your opponent is humiliated and fired. (And Fergie wonders why some managers won't have a drink with him after a game?)

C'MON REF!

The Guardian

Manchester United boss Sir Alex Ferguson in row with refs again

The Daily Telegraph

Sir Alex rant over referee Alan Wiley likely to see him land FA charge

DAILY Mirror

FERGUSON HITS OUT AT REFEREE CLATTENBURG AFTER UNITED HELD

THE INDEPENDENT

Ferguson in trouble again with FA over referee rage

FERGUSON LAUNCHES A FURIOUS TIRADE AT REF MIKE DEAN

ootball is a blame game. When you lose, it's much easier to point the finger at someone else than to take the rap yourself. And Sir Alex Ferguson's favourite scapegoat has always been the easiest target of them all — the referees.

If you believe the headlines, like those above, Fergie is convinced his Manchester United players are the greatest victims in world football. He'll have you believe they're regularly denied the glory they deserve by incompetent or dishonest officials.

It's utter nonsense, of course. But, in a broader sense, constantly moaning about referees is actually quite clever. It plants a seed. In the same way a casual comment from Fergie can upset the rhythm and confidence of a rival player or coach, it can also turn up the heat on a referee.

In the back of a referee's mind, he must surely know that if he errs on the side of caution when it comes to Manchester United he will avoid being publicly lambasted by the most influential manager in football.

If just once per season a referee thinks twice about awarding a penalty or a red card against United, then the little psychological trick is entirely worthwhile. Similarly, if United get the better of a few fifty-fifty decisions in a match, or an extra minute of injury time when they're behind, they have an advantage. It could be the difference between winning the title and falling short.

Of course there's no real way to measure whether Fergie has achieved anything with his bellyaching about referees but, as a general policy, continually slagging them has done little to harm his cause.

Sir Alex Ferguson's favourite
SCAPEGOAT has always
been the easiest target of them all –
↘ **THE REFEREES.**

FERGIE vs THE REFS

• *"I cannot believe the decision. Okay, it is human error, but it was one of the worst in my lifetime."*
Understatement has never been one of Fergie's strong points. When Darren Fletcher was harshly booked for diving in a 3—3 Champions League draw with CSKA Moscow in 2009 (instead of being awarded the penalty which replays suggested he deserved), Fergie decided it was one of the worst decisions he'd seen... ever.

• *"Back to your usual self Jeff. Fucking useless."*
One of Ferguson's many run-ins with referee Jeff Winter. The pair's most famous clash came when Winter was the fourth official in a 2003 Premier League game between Manchester United and Newcastle United. After aiming a foul-mouthed barrage at Winter, Ferguson was sent to the stands by referee Uriah Rennie. In his biography, *Who's The B*****d In Black*, Winter wrote that Fergie "drives me nuts — an absolute prat".

• *"He couldn't get up the pitch when the second goal was scored. He was telling Wayne Rooney he needed a rest. (He is) just not fit enough to referee a game of that standard — just not fit enough. It is an indictment of our game."*
After a lucky 2—2 draw with Sunderland in 2009, Fergie took out his frustration on 49-year-old referee Alan Wiley, accusing him of taking 30 seconds to caution players just so he could catch his breath.

• *"Managers get sacked because of things like that and he's going to referee a game next week."*
When Portsmouth pulled off a shock 1—0 victory over United in the quarter final of the 2007-08 FA Cup, Fergie blamed referee Martin Atkinson. The official awarded Portsmouth a penalty and sent off goal keeper Tomasz Kuszczak under the 'last man rule', even though Wayne Rooney and Anderson were standing on the goal line.

• *"At times he favoured Arsenal. Their second goal came from him not giving a free kick for a foul on Louis Saha on the far side. It should have been a foul for us."*
After watching Arsenal fight back for a draw with an injury time equaliser at the Emirates in November 2007, Fergie vented his spleen at referee Howard Webb.

• *"The referee saw it, he clearly saw it. He's elbowed him in the face and he's clearly in line with the actual incident. And I'm disappointed because he has stopped the game twice before that... that decision cost us the game, really."*
You'd swear he was talking about the Champions League final. In fact, this was Fergie's reaction to the refereeing in the Community Shield, 2009-10.

• *"Some referees don't like it. They don't like the truth but I just told him how bad he was in the first-half."*
Ferguson blasted Mark Clattenburg for failing to protect his players in a physical match against Bolton on 24 November, 2007. Exactly what he said to Clattenburg was never made public, but it was serious enough to warrant another punishment by the FA.

FERGIE'S
RAP SHEET

FEB 2011
Charge: Improper conduct
Details: Criticised referee Martin Atkinson following
United's 2-1 defeat at Chelsea
Penalty: 5 match ban
Fined: £30,000

NOV 2009
Charge: Gross improper conduct
Details: Used "wholly inappropriate" language in
verbal attack on referee Alan Wiley's fitness
Penalty: 4 match ban (2 suspended)
Fined £20,000
Issued public apology

NOV 2008
Charge: Improper conduct
Details: Rushed onto the pitch to confront referee
Mike Dean
Penalty: 2 match ban
Fined £10,000

DEC 2007
Charge: Misconduct
Details: Used abusive/insulting language towards
match official Mark Clattenburg
Penalty: 2 match ban
Fined £5,000

MAY 2003
Charge: Criticised UEFA
Details: Said the Champions League draw was fixed
to favour Italian and Spanish teams
Penalty: Fined Chf10,000

OCT 2003
Charge: Improper conduct
Details: Used abusive/insulting language towards
fourth official Jeff Winter
Penalty: 2 match ban
Fined £10,000

Sir Alex Ferguson lives in a
parallel universe, where

TIME
↘ MYSTERIOUSLY
SLOWS DOWN

if the Red Devils are trailing
and speeds up when they're
in front.

FERGIE TIME

Ask a fan of any club (other than Manchester United) and they'll tell you: Old Trafford is the Twilight Zone.

In fact, rival fans swear that Sir Alex Ferguson lives in a parallel universe, where time mysteriously slows down if the Red Devils are trailing and speeds up when they're in front.

It's an extraordinary phenomenon which, believe it or not, does have some scientific basis. A study of 1,140 matches between 2006 and 2009 found the team which played the smallest amount of injury time when leading in a home match was none other than Manchester United.

It prompted a headline in *The Times*: "It's a Fact! Fergie Time Does Exist in the Premier League".

If you switch on your television without knowing the score in a Manchester United game and you see Fergie tapping his watch on the sidelines, you can be sure United are in front. For every additional thirty seconds, Fergie's face turns a brighter shade of claret.

The most celebrated case of 'Fergie Time' came in the first thrilling Manchester derby of 2009-10 when Michael Owen scored the winner in a 4—3 victory for United at Old Trafford. The goal came in the ninety-sixth minute, even though fourth official Alan Wiley indicated there would be just four additional minutes. City boss Mark Hughes was, understandably, livid.

How to be Ferocious like Fergie:

⬎ Referees are not human. They don't have feelings, family or friends. They should never make mistakes. Condemn them, denounce them and chastise them mercilessly at every opportunity. Criticise their talent, fitness, integrity, impartiality and sanity. Remember, they're just another impediment standing between you and the glory you deserve.

⬎ As the oldest and longest-serving manager in the history of planet Earth, you should decide when a match starts and finishes. Don't be fooled into thinking there should be five minutes of injury time just because there were four goals, six substitutions and a seven minute delay for an injury. You're 1—0 ahead — there should be two minutes added.

REFEREES ARE
NOT HUMAN.⬋
They don't have feelings,
family or friends.

THE GREATEST EVER?

> Alex Ferguson is the best manager I've ever had at this level. Well, he's the only manager I've actually had at this level.

— DAVID BECKHAM, 2001

Measuring greatness can be an awfully tricky business.

In any sport, a coach or manager can be the world's most sought-after tactical genius one day, an unemployed laughing stock the next.

It only takes one bad season or — given today's demand for instant gratification — one bad month and a manager's world can come crashing down around him in a haze of nasty headlines and public humiliation.

Even Sir Alex Ferguson's gilt-edged world has, on occasion, come close to caving in.

Over the years he's been accused of being past his use-by date. He's been written off as old-fashioned and inflexible. His age, judgement and mental capacity have all been questioned by a salacious tabloid media who thrive on even a hint of managerial blood, especially that of the biggest manager of them all.

But, in two and a half decades with his backside on the hottest of Premier League hot seats, his blood has never spilled. It's boiled from time to time, but never spilled.

In lean times, his response to trash talk has always been the same: he vehemently defends himself, his players and his club. Then he backs it up with silverware — often having put *the club's* money where *his* mouth is.

> The game has changed a lot, on and off the pitch, since I joined the club in 1986. There was no freedom of contract. The press intensity was not as severe. Agents weren't as prominent. I had eight staff when I started here. Now I've got more staff than Marks and Spencer.
>
> **— SIR ALEX FERGUSON**

By any criteria, Sir Alex Ferguson does have a genuine claim to be considered not only great, but *the* greatest manager of all.

His collection of trophies is unsurpassed. His longevity is legendary. The average life span of a Premier League manager is just over three years between hiring and firing. By that measure, Fergie has lived a dozen lives. His status as an icon is beyond repute.

Luckily for him, football is not a popularity contest. It is, as they say, a results business — the ultimate results business. Whether you're counting trophies, analysing win-loss ratios or examining any of the myriad statistics meticulously recorded by football geeks worldwide, Sir

Alex's record defies comparison and, ultimately, vindicates him against those who criticise his methods.

Quite simply, he is the most successful manager in the history of the beautiful game, having dominated the most competitive league in the world for a generation.

His legacy can be measured by much more than cups and medals. Already many of those whose careers he shaped as players have become top-flight managers in their own right.

FERGIE'S TOP TEN PROTÉGÉS
Players who became EPL or SPL managers

1	Gordon Strachan – Coventry City, Southampton, Celtic, Middlesbrough
2	Steve Bruce – Birmingham City, Wigan, Sunderland
3	Mark Hughes – Blackburn Rovers, Manchester City, Fulham
4	Alex McLeish – Motherwell, Hibernian, Rangers, Scotland, Birmingham City, Aston Villa
5	Roy Keane – Sunderland, Ipswich Town
6	Paul Ince – Blackburn Rovers
7	Bryan Robson – Middlesbrough, West Bromwich, Thailand
8	Lauren Blanc – Bordeaux, France
9	Mark McGhee – Leicester City, Motherwell, Aberdeen
10	Willie Miller – Aberdeen

Despite everything Sir Alex has achieved, broad support for his right to claim a place among football's all-time greats was a long time coming. It was often written that he could not be compared to his idol Jock Stein until he won more domestic titles... or sit alongside continental greats like Marcello Lippi or Giovanni Trapattoni until he claimed at least two European Cups.

Eventually, he ticked both boxes.

But even as the titles piled up, pundits and journalists continued to leave him off their 'best ever' lists, despite having won far more trophies than many of those ranked above him. That was long ago. Now, through sheer weight of numbers and years, he's never left off such honour rolls. Yet there is still an underlying hint of reluctance from those who chronicle his greatness.

But why? In some cases it is personal. There's no way to say this nicely (and by now you've got the idea) but, quite frankly, he's pissed a lot of people off over the years. He's attacked journalists and pundits as a matter of course, sometimes physically but — more terrifyingly — verbally.

There are football-related arguments, too. The first (and most often used against him) is that during most of his United career he's been able to buy almost any player he wants, as manager of the world's richest and most popular football club. The revenue from sales of replica Beckham or Ronaldo shirts when they were United pin-up boys would have paid for an entire club at the other end of the Premier League table.

	FORBES MAGAZINE 10 MOST VALUABLE SPORTS FRANCHISES 2010	
		Value (USD)
1	Manchester United	1.835 billion
2	Dallas Cowboys	1.650 billion
3	New York Yankees	1.600 billion
4	Washington Redskins	1.550 billion
5	New England Patriots	1.361 billion
6	Real Madrid	1.323 billion
7	New York Giants	1.183 billion
8	Arsenal	1.181 billion
9	New York Jets	1.170 billion
10	Houston Texans	1.150 billion

There's more. Aside from a brief stint as Scotland manager following the untimely death of Jock Stein, Sir Alex has always been a club manager, where there are three or more major trophies up for grabs each season. Managers who have spent large parts of their careers working with national teams, like Guus Hiddink or Luiz Felipe Scolari, only have one major trophy every two or four years to aim for. It would be a pretty harsh argument to sustain, but it could be contested that Fergie's managerial CV will never be complete without football's ultimate prize, the World Cup.

Also, Ferguson went into management at the age of 32 and he's still going well past retirement age. That gives him a ten-year head start on those who played until their late thirties then spent five or six years learning the ropes as an assistant, as most managers do these days.

As the epic story of football is written and rewritten, numerous managers with far fewer trophies in their cabinets than Fergie are remembered with a wistful romanticism, a kind of misty-eyed passion which will never be applied to the stern Scotsman.

While Fergie can claim credit for resurrecting United as a power, it's been suggested that his European successes are nothing compared to those of Brian Clough, who took unfashionable Nottingham Forest to back-to-back European Cups.

The man whose shadow from which Fergie emerged at the Theatre of Dreams, Sir Matt Busby, built an extraordinary team of youngsters known as 'Busby's Babes' in the 1950s. His team claimed the League titles of 1955-56 and 1956-57 before the horrific air disaster of 6 February, 1958. Tragically, eight of his young stars were killed when the plane carrying the United team back from a European Cup match in Belgrade skidded off a Munich runway. The crash almost cost Busby his own life.

Despite the horror and agony of Munich, Busby rebuilt the team almost from scratch. Miraculously, under his guidance, United won two more titles and, the ultimate, the European Cup. It is arguably the greatest football story ever told.

Other managers have won their place in history for the style their teams have displayed, rather than the number of trophies they have won — most notably, the creator of *total football* Rinus Michels and its defensive equivalent, *catenaccio*, invented by Helenio Herrera. Michels' Ajax and Holland teams played what is widely regarded as the most beautiful, fluid football ever played (although Holland fell just short at the 1974 World Cup). Herrera's Inter Milan enjoyed great success with the bolted-door *catenaccio* style of defending, which changed the face of football in Italy.

The list on the following page, of the most successful managers in history, contains *nearly* all the best-known managerial maestros from right around the world. But there are notable absences, like Vicente Del Bosque, who's won two Champions Leagues trophies, two La Liga crowns and the small matter of the 2010 World Cup.

It seems absurd to look at that collection of greats and not see Bill Shankly's name among them, either. He won just three League titles and two FA Cups at Liverpool, nowhere near enough for a place among the silverware superstars. But most good football judges rate him among the top ten managers in English history. After all, he took the Reds from the bottom of the second division and laid the foundations for a golden period (under Bob Paisley) in the 1970s and '80s, almost equal to United's dominance of the 1990s and first decade of the 2000s.

Similarly, another World Cup-winning manager is missing: Germany's 'Der Kaiser', Franz Beckenbauer, who won only one German and one French league title in club football, but is widely regarded as among the greatest football thinkers of his time.

It all goes to show that while statistics certainly tell a story, they don't always tell the whole story.

THE TROPHY KINGS

This list only includes major trophies at an elite level. It does not include second-tier competitions like the Europa League or even the Cup Winners Cup. It does not include lower division titles or one-off matches like the Charity Shield or various 'Super Cups'. Like all such compilations, it has been compiled with a degree of subjectivity. In some South American leagues there is more than one title on offer in a given year and several Cup competitions which, it could be argued, are no easier to win than the FA Cup. It only includes trophies won before July 2011.

31 **SIR ALEX FERGUSON** — 2 Champions Leagues, 12 English Leagues, 5 FA Cups, 4 League Cups, 3 Scottish Leagues, 4 Scottish Cups, 1 Scottish League Cup

30 **WILLIE MALEY** — 16 Scottish Leagues, 14 Scottish Cups

30 **BILL STRUTH** — 18 Scottish Leagues, 10 Scottish Cups, 2 Scottish League Cups

26   **JOCK STEIN** — 1 European Cup, 10 Scottish Leagues, 9 Scottish Cups, 6 Scottish League Cups

22   **VALERIY LOBANOVSKIY** — 8 USSR Leagues, 6 USSR Cups, 5 Ukrainian Leagues, 3 Ukrainian Cups

17   **OTTMAR HITZFELD** — 2 Champions Leagues, 7 German Leagues, 3 German Cups, 2 Swiss Leagues, 3 Swiss Cups

16   **ERNST HAPPEL** — 2 European Cups, 2 German Leagues, 1 German Cup, 2 Austrian Leagues, 1 Austrian Cup, 2 Dutch Leagues, 2 Dutch Cups, 3 Belgian Leagues, 1 Belgian Cup

16   **JOSE MOURINHO** — 2 Champions Leagues, 2 English Leagues, 2 FA Cups, 2 League Cups, 1 Spanish Cup, 2 Portuguese Leagues, 2 Portuguese Cups, 2 Italian Leagues, 1 Italian Cup

15   **GIOVANNI TRAPATTONI** — 1 European Cup, 7 Italian Leagues, 2 Italian Cups, 1 German League, 1 German Cup, 1 German League Cup, 1 Portuguese League title, 1 Austrian League title

14   **MIGUEL MUNOZ** — 2 European Cups, 9 Spanish Leagues, 3 Spanish Cups

14   **KARL RAPPAN** — 6 Swiss Leagues, 8 Swiss Cups

13   **BOB PAISLEY** — 3 European Cups, 6 English Leagues, 3 League Cups

12 **SVEN-GORAN ERIKSSON** — 1 Swedish League, 2 Swedish Cups, 3 Portuguese Leagues, 1 Portuguese Cup, 1 Italian League, 4 Italian Cups

12 **HELENIO HERRERA** — 2 European Cups, 4 Spanish Leagues, 2 Spanish Cups, 3 Italian Leagues, 1 Italian Cup

12 **GUUS HIDDINK** — 1 European Cup, 6 Dutch Leagues, 4 Dutch Cups, 1 FA Cup

12 **UDO LATTEK** — 1 European Cup, 8 German Leagues, 3 German Cups

12 **RINUS MICHELS** — 1 Euro Championships, 1 European Cup, 1 Spanish League, 1 Spanish Cup, 4 Dutch Leagues, 3 Dutch Cups, 1 German Cup

11 **ALBERT BATTEUX** — 9 French Leagues, 2 French Cups

11 **CARLOS BIANCHI** — 7 Argentine Leagues, 4 Copa Libertadores

11 **LOUIS VAN GAAL** — 1 Champions League, 4 Dutch Leagues, 1 Dutch Cup, 2 Spanish Leagues, 1 Spanish Cup, 1 German League, 1 German Cup

10 **HENNES WEISWEILER** — 4 German Leagues, 3 German Cups, 1 Swiss League, 1 Swiss Cup, 1 North American League

10 **ARSENE WENGER** — 3 English Leagues, 4 FA Cups, 1 French League, 1 French Cup, 1 Japanese Cup

9   **CARLOS ALBERTO PARREIRA** — 1 World Cup, 1 Copa America, 2 Asian Cups, 2 Brazilian leagues, 1 Brazilian Cup, 1 Turkish League, 1 Ghanaian League

8   **SIR MATT BUSBY** — 1 European Cup, 5 English Leagues, 2 FA Cups,

8   **FABIO CAPELLO** — 1 Champions League, 5 Italian Leagues, 2 Spanish Leagues

8   **BRIAN CLOUGH** — 2 European Cups, 2 English Leagues, 4 League Cups

8   **BELA GUTTMANN** — 2 European Cups, 2 Hungarian Leagues, 3 Portuguese Leagues, 1 Portuguese Cup

8   **MARCELLO LIPPI** — 1 World Cup, 1 Champions League, 5 Italian Leagues, 1 Italian Cup

8   **MARIO ZAGALLO** — 1 World Cup, 1 Copa America, 5 Brazilian Leagues, 1 Brazilian Cup

7   **JOHAN CRUYFF** — 1 European Cup, 4 Spanish Leagues, 1 Spanish Cup, 2 Dutch Cups

7   **OTTO REHHAGEL** — 1 Euro Championship, 3 German Leagues, 3 German Cups

7   **NEREO ROCCO** — 2 European Cups, 2 Italian Leagues, 3 Italian Cups

7   **LUIZ FELIPE SCOLARI** — 1 World Cup, 1 Brazilian League, 3 Brazilian Cups, 1 Cop Libertadores, 1 Uzbek League

Fergie is the last old-style Gaffer in the business. It's fair to suggest that when Sir Alex goes, an entire managerial style will go with him. Who else could get away with giving players a clip over the ear when they misbehave?

He still rules with an iron fist. Without a hint of immodesty, he'll tell you the manager remains by far the most important man at any football club — ahead of individual megastar players or highly-paid marketing gurus.

Fear and intimidation remain key weapons in his arsenal. Despite players' outlandish salaries and celebrity lifestyles, he is still very much a father figure to them... placing limits on their social activities and, as we've seen, happy to demand they get a haircut or pull up their baggy trousers.

For all his strengths and weakness, Fergie is nothing if not effective. His public image is a world away from the private man described by those who know him best. Close friends characterise him as warm and generous, possessing a wicked sense of humour. The rest of the world only catches an occasional glimpse of that Sir Alex.

He is still very much a **FATHER FIGURE** ↙ to them… placing limits on their social activities and, as we've seen, happy to demand they get a haircut or pull up their baggy trousers.

DON'T MENTION THE WAR

To say Fergie doesn't give a toss about political correctness is an understatement. He is the very antithesis of today's PC-obsessed society.

Case in point: his reaction to Manchester United's elimination from the 2009-10 Champions League at the hands of Bayern Munich. He was incensed that his young defender Rafael da Silva was sent off in the second leg at Old Trafford.

"They got him sent off — there's no doubt about that. They would have never won if we had eleven men. He is a young boy, inexperienced and there's a bit of immaturity about what happened, but they got him sent off," he roared.

But, as if that wasn't enough, he delivered his *coup de grace* and, yet again, landed himself in hot water:

"Typical Germans," he ranted.

Thank you Sir Alex Fawlty. What next — funny walks along the touchline?

As Fergie enters the eighth decade of an extraordinary life, he finds himself in the frustrating situation of being remembered — potentially — as Europe's "not quite" man.

Even before he'd completed the task of knocking Liverpool off their perch, Ferguson confessed a far greater ambition was to bridge the gap between Manchester United (three European Cups/Champions Leagues) and the big guns, Real Madrid (nine) and AC Milan (seven).

Yet rather than climb that table, United have now fallen behind Barcelona (four) and find themselves level with Inter Milan (three), despite making three finals in four years between 2008 and 2011.

Much like a golfer who peaked when Tiger Woods was at his invincible best, a tennis player whose best years coincided with Roger Federer's dominant era or one of many Formula One drivers who spent their careers in Michael Schumacher's dust, F C Barcelona loom as a genuine threat to Fergie's global legacy.

After brushing United aside in the 2009 Champions League final in Rome, Barcelona were even more ruthless at Wembley in 2011. The 3—1 thrashing simply emphasised the enormous gulf between the Spanish and English champions.

The Catalans are, without doubt, the greatest team of their generation. Of all the main contenders — including the two Milan teams, Real Madrid and Chelsea — Manchester United remain the next best.

But who remembers *next best*?

With all the money in the world, Fergie may be helpless to prevent Pep Guardiola's men from denying him the final piece of his golden jigsaw.

He was 69 at the time of the Wembley humiliation... players like Ryan Giggs, Rio Ferdinand and Paul Scholes were also in the twilight of their playing careers.

Respected football writer Oliver Holt hinted that it might be time to pack it in and give up.

"Why Fergie must be tempted to say 'What's the point in trying to beat this Barca side?' and retire," was the headline to Holt's article in *The Mirror*.

The fact that Fergie never asks "what's the point" is why he has survived so long.

There is always a point; a new target, a new bunch of kids to work with, a new trophy to strive for... in this case, perhaps, one final challenge.

In the face of such defeatism, you can't help but think Sir Alex Ferguson will probably do what he has always done — find a way to succeed.

He certainly doesn't talk like a man ready to give up.

"I have no plans to retire, I must say that," he said on the eve of the 2011 final.

"Cathy is delighted. She would have thrown me out, anyway."

"The salient point is that whilst my health is good, carry on. You hear many stories of people who come off the treadmill and their system breaks down. I don't want that happening to me."

"My father retired on his 65th birthday, and one year later he was dead."

It's obvious that football keeps Fergie young. In spite of his often Jurassic disposition, he can still communicate with boys a quarter his age. If anything, he commands more respect than ever.

In spite of his often **JURASSIC** ↘ **DISPOSITION,** he can still communicate with boys a quarter his age.

He still holds a magical ability to take a 20-year-old and transform him into a global football superstar who, without Fergie's guidance, may never have made it.

Spanish World Cup winner Gerard Pique is one of numerous players who describe Fergie as a father figure.

"When I arrived there I was seventeen and it was really hard for me to leave my family. He helped in all the ways, not only in football terms but also how to find a house and all my relations out of football. For me, Alex Ferguson will always be a second father," Pique says.

Cristiano Ronaldo is equally glowing: "I am planning to go to Manchester and say goodbye to Mr. Ferguson. He has been like a father to me. I have to thank him for all he has taught me — how to think things through and take decisions in my life. He has been one of the most important factors and influences in my career. He will always have a special place in my heart."

But the most significant relationship of Ferguson's managerial career has been with Ryan Giggs, his "floating Cocker Spaniel". Together, they have forged the greatest manager/player partnership the game has ever seen. When Giggs was 13 his father walked out on the family — the Welshman remains scarred by the unforgettable agony of having to carry his dad's bag to the bus stop the day he left.

But contrary to Fergie's great saying "where one door closes another slams in your face", the exit of Giggs' father, Danny Wilson, signaled the arrival of a new paternal influence in his life. Just a few months later he came under the spell of Sir Alex.

"I was awestruck by him. One of the first things he said to me was that I had all the coaches here to help me with football matters but, if I ever needed anything outside football, the door was always open. He helped me because that time was a tricky one for me. My mum and dad were splitting up and he knew that."

When Giggs' squeaky clean reputation was shattered in May 2011 with revelations of an affair with a reality television contestant, Ferguson was said to be devastated.

Despite that, Giggs — more than anyone — deserves the final word on Sir Alex Ferguson.

"He was and always will be the best manager in the world. He has always supported us and always encouraged us and that's why all his teams have achieved a lot of success. I wish him all the success and happiness for rest of his life."

How to be Ferocious like Fergie:

🡖 Sacrifice every fibre of your being to pursue a single cause. Put your wife, family, privacy, hobbies, interests and every aspect of your personal life second to your chosen calling. Accept you will be criticised by many and hated by some. There will be books written about you: some positive, some negative. Expect every move you make to be recorded and played back in slow motion, sometimes completely out of context. Every word you utter will be analysed and dissected to within an inch of its life. If you succeed, celebrate in any way you choose. It will all have been worth it. After all, you can forget all the cliches about football breaking down barriers, bringing cultures together and moving mankind forward... it is about one thing — winning. And nobody, nobody has done that more often than Sir Alexander Chapman Ferguson.

Expect every move you make to be

RECORDED and played back in slow motion, sometimes completely out of context. Every word you utter will be

🡖**ANALYSED AND DISSECTED** to within an inch of its life.

YOU KNOW YOU'VE MADE IT WHEN THEY'RE TELLING JOKES ABOUT YOU

What's the difference between Sir Alex Ferguson and God?
God doesn't think he's Sir Alex Ferguson.

What's the difference between Sir Alex Ferguson's post-match press conference and giving birth?
One is pure agony, the other is having a baby.

Wayne Rooney calls Sir Alex Ferguson and says he can't put together the jigsaw he got for Christmas. "The picture on the box is of a chicken, but the pieces don't fit together. If I can't do it by Saturday, boss, I won't be able to concentrate on the game," Rooney says.
In a panic, Fergie tells him to bring it to training and he'll give him a hand.
After training the next day, the pair are staring at the pieces on Fergie's desk when Ryan Giggs walks in... "What's with the cornflakes, Gaffer?"

Sir Alex Ferguson is invited to be a judge at the Miss Universe competition. Seeking his favour, Miss Italy sits on his lap, lowers the strap on her dress and asks him to sign her left breast, which he does. Miss Australia follows, lowers the strap on her dress and asks him to sign her right breast, which he does. Miss Argentina walks up, hands him a pen and lifts the front of her dress. Fergie leaps to his feet, throws down the pen and shouts "No, no, no... last time I signed an Argentinean twat it cost me £28 million!"

How does Sir Alex Ferguson change a light bulb?
He holds it in the air and the world revolves around him.

Sir Alex Ferguson and Arsene Wenger are standing before God who is sitting on his throne at the Pearly Gates.
"Before granting you a place in heaven, I must first ask you what you believe in," God declares.
"What do you believe, my son?" he asks Wenger.
Arsene looks God in the eye and says, "I believe football to be the food of life. Nothing else brings such unbridled joy to so many people."
God wipes a tear from his eye with his Arsenal shirt and offers Wenger a place in Heaven.
He then turns to Ferguson.
"And you, Mr. Ferguson, what do you believe in?"
"I believe," Fergie says, "You're in my seat..."

ABOUT THE AUTHOR

Glenn Connley is the face and voice of European football in Singapore. He is best known as the presenter of *FC Daily*, the Football Channel's nightly flagship news program.

Prior to that he experienced every sports broadcaster's dream; anchoring the iconic ESPN news powerhouse *SportsCenter*, across Asia and the Indian subcontinent. Glenn was Head of Production for ESPN's 24-hour news channel, *ESPNews*, when it launched in 2010.

Glenn's career began in Melbourne, Australia, in 1990, when he joined Australia's biggest-selling newspaper, the *Herald Sun*, as a cadet reporter at the age of 17. Five years later he joined the city's top-rating radio station, 3AW, as newsreader and crime reporter.

Glenn moved into television in 1997, working as a producer, presenter and reporter at a number of Australia's top news and current affairs programs, including the long-running *Today Tonight* on the Seven Network and *A Current Affair* at Channel Nine.

Glenn's great passions are sport and travel. His most heartfelt sporting affections are shared between AFL team, Richmond, and a certain Premier League team in blue. He enjoys golf (he's a regular commentator on the Asian Tour), kickboxing, swimming and running. He has walked among lions in a Zimbabwe national park, run with the bulls in Pamplona, Spain, and trekked the Himalayas of Nepal.

He lives with his wife, Jane, in Singapore.

PHOTO CREDITS

SOURCES

Back From The Brink — Paul McGrath (with Vincent Hogan), Arrow Books 2006

Cantona: The Rebel Who Would Be King — Philippe Auclair, Pan McMillan 2009

Dalglish - My Autobiography — Kenny Dalglish & Henry Winter, Hodder & Staughton 1996

Gordon Strachan: The Biography — Leo Moynihan, Worldwide Books 2004

Head to Head — Jaap Stam, Harper Collins 2001

Managing My Life — Sir Alex Ferguson (with Hugh McIlvanney), Hodder & Staughton 1999.

My Defence: Winning, Losing, Scandals and the drama of Germany 2006 — Ashley Cole, Headline Book Publishing, 2006

My Idea Of Fun — Lee Sharpe, Orion 2005

The Boss — Many Sides of Alex Ferguson — Michael Crick, Simon & Schuster 2002

*Who's the B*****d in Black?* — Jeff Winter, Ebury Press, 2006